PREACH

DELIVER

C000052808

*Captivate Your Audience,
Kill Bad Habits, and Master
the Art of Sermon Delivery*

by Brandon Hilgemann

Copyright

Preach and Deliver: Captivate Your Audience, Kill Bad Habits, and Master the Art of Sermon Delivery / by Brandon Hilgemann

Copyright © 2016 by Brandon Hilgemann, Pro-Preacher.com. All rights reserved. First Edition.

For more information, go to ProPreacher.com

Dedication

To my kids, Ashlyn and Jaxon. May you both continue to grow to love Christ with all your heart, soul, mind, and strength.

Contents

INTRODUCTION: The What and the How

The general history of the world surely demon-strates quite plainly that the men who truly made history have been men who could speak, who could deliver a message, and who could get people to act as the result of the effect they produced upon them.

— Martyn Lloyd-Jones[1]

---

[1] D. Martin Lloyd-Jones, *Preaching and Preachers* (Grand Rapids: Zondervan, 2011), 20.

I stood in terror in a musty youth room of an old church. Seventeen teenagers stared at me with blank expressions.

It was Wednesday night. I was a freshman in Bible college, invited to preach for a local youth pastor who was out of town. I wouldn't doubt it if I was his last option after asking everyone else he could.

There I stood. All eyes on me. Sweat pouring from my forehead. My hands shook. My knees knocked. And my voice trembled as I read my sermon word-for-word from my notes.

My eyes never left the page. With white knuckles, my right hand gripped the microphone. My left hand held my manuscript as if it were my only hope of survival. My feet might as well have been cemented to the floor because they never moved.

Those poor teenagers. How they did not fall asleep or walk out I will never know.

I could not have preached worse. The message was OK, but the delivery was painful.

Preaching has a dual nature. It rests on two pillars: the *what* and the *how*. The *what* is the content—the words you say. The *how* is the delivery—the way you communicate the words.

Preaching is both *what* you say, and *how* you say it. We often know the *what* but neglect the *how*. My first sermon sure did.

If you are like most pastors, you've spent years of your life learning the content for your sermon. We go to Bible College and Seminary to learn the Bible. We take classes on theology, Biblical interpretation, church history, and maybe even Greek or Hebrew. We know our Bibles. We know the *what*.

But here's the problem: **Most preaching fails not for lack of content, but for deficient delivery.** If you preach biblically-based sermons, you have the content. We graduate with diplomas about the *what* but haven't mastered the *how*.

No matter how good your message, if your delivery is poor, your audience won't receive the message. Even a great message with poor delivery will result in a bored, distracted, or even annoyed audience.

Famed playwright George Bernard Shaw once said, "The single biggest problem in communication is the illusion that it has taken place." That's what happens when we give a message with poor delivery. We think we communicated because we said the words, but it's an illusion. We had a good *what* and a bad *how*.

Communication is a two-way street. You must do everything in your power to remove potential roadblocks. To do that, we need to go back to the basics of sermon delivery.

Back to the Basics

In 1959, Vince Lombardi was hired to be the head football coach of the Green Bay Packers. He took the difficult task of turning around a losing franchise.

After a miserable game, the players gathered in the locker room in silence. They braced themselves for Lombardi to enter and erupt in a verbal assault.

After a few moments, Lombardi entered the room with a football in his hands. He stood in silence, searching for words. The players prepared for the worst.

Lombardi lifted the football and broke the silence with one of the greatest quotes in NFL history: "Gentlemen, this is a football!"

He proceeded to explain the boundaries of a football field, the length of the goal line, and how moving the ball across the goal line scores six points. Lombardi brought a room full of pros back to the most basic elements of the game.

Those five, legendary words defined Lombardi's legacy as a coach. He never stopped focusing his team on the basics. He demanded perfection in the smallest fundamentals of the game—like the proper form for blocking and tackling.

After years of losing, Lombardi took the Packers to win five championships in seven years—including Super Bowl I and II.

In fact, the Packers never had a losing season under Lombardi. He is regarded as one of the greatest coaches of all time. He left such a legacy that the NFL named the Super Bowl trophy in his honor, the Lombardi Trophy. All this resulted because Lombardi took his struggling team back to the basics.

I tell you this not only because my family brainwashed me at a young age to be a diehard Packers fan, but also because we could learn from Lombardi. We need to get back to the basics of preaching. We need to refocus on the fundamentals of sermon delivery.

What are the essential components of good sermon delivery? The rest of this book will attempt to answer this question.

In my years of education on a bachelors and masters level from great Christian institutions, I learned the message of the Bible. But I didn't learn how to deliver that message.

My prayer is that this book helps you to think through the way you deliver a sermon—the nuances of body language, eye contact, gestures, and more—so that you can preach the gospel in a powerful way that grips the hearts and minds of your audience.

In my first book, *Preaching Nuts & Bolts: Conquer Sermon Prep, Save Time, and Write Better Messages*, I wrote about the art of sermon preparation. It teaches the fundamentals of the what. This book is about the how. Once you have the message written, how can you deliver it in the most effective way?

If you need help writing the sermon, you may want to start with my first book. For this book, I will assume that you already wrote a good message, and we will focus on how to deliver it.

The Commitment

I want to be honest with you upfront. I hesitated writing this book. Writing about sermon delivery seems a bit odd. Doesn't it?

You cannot see my eye contact or body language as I type at my desk. I can teach you through these words, but there is only so much you can improve by learning about sermon delivery if you don't practice what you learn.

Preaching is like playing a sport; you have to practice the fundamentals and review the game film to identify areas that need more practice. You will never be done. Every week you need to practice, evaluate, and practice again. Michael Jordan, Wayne Gretzky, Peyton Manning, and Tiger Woods never graduated from practice. Even at the top of their game, they all had coaches to help them refine their fundamentals.

This book will help you learn about the basics of sermon delivery, but reading alone will not make you better. That's why at the end of every section, I have included an action step. Think of it as a challenge to apply what you learned in the chapter.

Also, you need to understand that this book assumes that you realize that God is ultimately in control. Preaching is an awesome partnership between the preacher and God. If God is not involved in your preaching, little will get done. This book is full of practical advice to help you do everything in your power to improve. But without God, you can be the most polished speaker in the world and completely miss the mark.

So stop right now and pray. Ask God to guide you through this process as you work to become a more clear and effective communicator for Him.

Go on. Do it.

If you truly want to improve your sermon delivery, reading this book is not enough. It's a start, but first, you need God. Second, you must practice what you learn. And third, you need to evaluate every sermon you preach.

As Charles Spurgeon, the "Prince of Preachers," taught his students:

Get a friend to tell you your faults, or better still, welcome an enemy who will watch you keenly and sting you savagely. What a blessing such an irritating critic will be to a wise man, what an intolerable nuisance to a fool! Correct yourself diligently and frequently, or you will fall into errors unawares, false tones will grow, and slovenly habits will form insensibly; therefore criticize yourself with unceasing care.[2]

You can and should evaluate your sermons on your own. But, I highly suggest recruiting people to

---

[2] Charles H. Spurgeon, *Lectures To My Students* (Fig, 2012), 123.

help you evaluate your preaching. It will be one of the most painful things you ever do, but you will grow faster than you could ever do alone. Other people will see things you can't.

In summary, I am asking you to commit to three things if you want to grow as a preacher. First, commit this next season of your life to a healthy relationship with Christ. Second, commit to taking action on what you learn in this little book. And third, commit to evaluating your sermons.

If you do, I guarantee that your sermon delivery will improve.

Are you in? If so, here's your first step.

ACTION STEP: Download Your Free Sermon Evaluation Guide

In my desire to help you practice and evaluate your preaching, I have created a free sermon evaluation guide based on the content of this book.

Go to www.ProPreacher.com/Deliver to download your free guide.

This evaluation guide is a summary of what you will learn in this book. In nearly every chapter, I will ask you to work on a specific aspect of your preaching and evaluate it in your next sermon. Use this evaluation form after every sermon to help identify the areas you need to improve the most.

And if you really want to get better, give copies to a few people you trust and ask them to evaluate your sermon too. Community is a powerful motivator. So find people that will encourage you about your strengths and hold you accountable to improve your weaknesses.

1. AUTHENTICITY: Be The Same on Stage and Off

The man, the whole man, lies behind the sermon. Preaching is not the performance of an hour. It is the outflow of a life. It takes twenty years to make a sermon, because it takes twenty years to make the man.

— E. M. Bounds[3]

It's rare these days to find a pastor who has devoted a lifetime of faithful service to a single church. But I have had the pleasure of knowing two different

---

[3]   E.M. Bounds, *Power Through Prayer* (London: Marshall, Morgan & Scott, 1912), 11.

pastors who faithfully ministered to their churches for over 30 years.

In the last year, I watched both of these men retire from their position as senior pastor. As I attended the services to honor these men and all that they have accomplished, a similar phrase caught my ear: "He was the same person off the stage as he was on it."

They served in different cities, had different personalities, and weren't perfect. But both of these men were authentic. What you saw was what you got. They faithfully served God in every area of their life.

Is there anything better we could ask for in a preacher? There may be no greater quality in preaching than authenticity.

Nobody wants to listen to a preacher who feels like a used car salesperson, trying to push them to do or buy something. People are longing for a leader who is authentic—someone who lives, sleeps, and breathes what they preach.

Authenticity is not something that you can teach. It's not a tactic. It's not a trick. Authenticity is not something you do; it's who you are.

If you perfect all the other elements of this book but are not authentic, you will fail to connect with your audience. You will be no more than an actor on a stage, pretending to be something you are not. And people will see through your charade.

You have probably run into these types of preachers before. They may be a charismatic speaker. They may look the part and have a smooth presentation. But inside, they are an empty shell. The sermon is just polished words in a slick suit, but there is something about it that doesn't feel right.

You don't get the sense that the person is practicing what they preach. You don't get the feeling that they buy what they're selling. Although you may not be able to put your finger on exactly what it is, there is a disconnect somewhere. It doesn't feel authentic.

In the book *The Challenge of Preaching*, John Stott writes, "People expect high standards of honesty from preachers and sniff around like dogs after a rat to see if they can discover any contradictions in us."[4] As a preacher, your life is in the public eye. People will judge you on everything you say and do.

In the introduction, I said that preaching rests on two pillars: the what and the how. The what is the content—the words you say. The how is the delivery—the way you communicate the words. But there is also

---

[4]   John Stott, *The Challenge of Preaching*, Kindle ed. (Cambridge: Wm. B. Eerdmans, 2013), Location 1298.

a third, almost hidden pillar that stands behind the other two. The third pillar is the who. The who is the preacher—the type of person you are.

Who delivers the message is as important as what is said and how you say it. Just as you wouldn't listen to Hitler give a lecture on loving your neighbor, people won't listen to a preacher who doesn't live what they teach. If a person's life contradicts their message, nobody listens.

The most important thing you can do for your preaching is to be the same person on stage that you are off of it. Far too many pastors fall because their private life doesn't line up with their preaching life.

Authentic preachers live their sermons. They stand on the stage, rip open their chest, and reveal their heart to the congregation. Everything they say and do comes from deep within them. It's not an act. It's not a show. It's not a presentation. Authentic preachers bleed their soul.

Six Elements of Authentic Preaching

Although you cannot force authenticity, there are some elements that contribute to authentic preaching:

passion, transparency, compassion, conviction, urgency, and confidence.

1. Passion

The best preachers are passionate. They preach with a sense of anticipation of the amazing work God might do in His people through His Word.

If you are not excited about what you are saying, how can you expect anyone else to be? It's tragic to make the most amazing story ever told boring.

Get fired up about the message. Bottle it up. Let it stir within you all week so that by Sunday (or whenever you preach), you can't contain it anymore. The message explodes out of you.

Nobody wants to listen to a passionless preacher. You must believe in what you are saying so strongly that you cannot help but get excited when talking about it. Your true personality shines through.

Your passion will be visible in your body language. When you are passionate about something, you move. Think about your body language the last time you had a heated argument, comforted a crying child, or watched your team win in the final seconds of the game. You were so moved that you moved. *(We will talk more about body language in the next chapter.)*

15

In the book *Christ-Centered Preaching*, Bryan Chapell says that "no set of delivery dos and don'ts supersedes the power of caring deeply about what you say... Showing genuine enthusiasm for what you deeply believe is the only unbreakable rule of great delivery."[5]

2. Transparency

If you want to be authentic, you have to be real with people. Let people know that you are not perfect. Share stories of how you have failed. Talk about how you've been personally convicted of something recently. Let people know that following Jesus is not easy, even for the preacher.

When you are transparent, your humanity shows. You are a regular person like everyone else with quirks, flaws, and struggles. So don't take yourself too seriously.

Be vulnerable about shortcomings in your life. Don't pretend like you have it all together. Tell us where you struggle. Tell us that you aren't perfect. Let us know how you are wrestling with your sermon's topic.

---

5   Bryan Chapell, *Christ-Centered Preaching: Redeeming the Expository Sermon*, Kindle ed. (Grand Rapids: Baker, 2015), Location 7584.

Like Tim Keller says, "You should be something like a clear glass through which people can see a gospel-changed soul in such a way that they want it too, and so that they get a sense of God's presence as well."[6]

3. Compassion

Loving to preach and loving those we preach are two very different things. You need to know your audience. What are their greatest pains, fears, failures, and struggles? When you know your audience, your preaching will naturally flow out of your compassion for them.

It doesn't matter how well you preach, without love you are just making a noise (1 Corinthians 13:1). But when you preach with love for your people, people can feel it. And like a father who warns his child not to play in the street, you can warn your people of the dangerous things they are messing around with, and they will know that you are only saying it out of love.

---

6   Timothy Keller, *Preaching: Communicating Faith in an Age of Skepticism*, Kindle ed. (New York: Penguin, 2015), Location 317.

Do you care about the people in your audience? Do you want nothing more than to help them? Is it obvious in the way you speak?

I've known pastors who love preaching, but not people. The best pastors preach with heartfelt compassion for their people.

4. Conviction

The best preachers have been personally convicted by the message God has given them long before they ever preach it.

As the Puritan theologian John Owen said, "No man preaches his sermon well to others if he doth not first preach it to his own heart."[7]

If the message has not changed you, it will not change your listeners. Let it challenge your life first. You can only lead your people as far as you have gone yourself.

Conviction is vital for authenticity. Your sermon won't just be theoretical talk. You will be preaching from experience. People will be able to feel that you actually practice what you preach. There is no greater example of a preacher who believed and followed his teachings than Jesus.

---

7 Charles H. Spurgeon, *Lectures To My Students* (Fig, 2012), 15.

Jesus didn't just teach on prayer; he often withdrew to pray (Luke 5:16). Jesus didn't just teach on loving sinners; he had dinner with them (Matthew 9:10-12). Jesus lived what he said. He didn't just talk a good talk, he walked the walk all the way through death on a cross.

You must believe what you are saying. With every fiber of your being, you have to know it is true. The greatest lessons we teach come from our lives, not our mouths.

5. Urgency

The best preachers have a sense of urgency. They feel the urgency of the gospel. They know that time is short and eternity is long.

We have a message that is the difference between life or death. The implications are Heaven or Hell. Our time is short. Life is a vapor. We never know if this will be our last message or theirs.

Martyn Lloyd-Jones, in his book *Preaching and Preachers,* writes, "You are not simply imparting information, you are dealing with souls, you are dealing with pilgrims on the way to eternity, you are dealing with matters not only of life and death in this world, but with eternal destiny. Nothing can be so terribly urgent."[8]

Authentic preachers know the urgency of the gospel. They don't pretend like the people listening have forever to make a decision. We are never guaranteed another moment. The time to act is now. If you believe the gospel, you will preach like there is no tomorrow, because one day you will be right.

6. Confidence

Authentic preachers are confident. They believe that God, through the power of the Holy Spirit, will speak through the proclamation of His Word.

Authentic preachers also know what they are talking about. They have studied the Bible. Its words are engrained on their hearts. They know the text they are preaching so well that they could preach without notes if needed. So their eyes are engaged and fully present in the moment.

If you struggle with confidence, remember, you can be confident because you are not preaching from your authority, but God's. You don't preach out of self-confidence, but confidence in the almighty, allknowing, unchanging God.

---

[8]   D. Martin Lloyd-Jones, *Preaching and Preachers* (Grand Rapids: Zondervan, 2011), 104.

We are an ambassador of Christ (2 Corinthians 5:20). We are representing Him. So place your confidence in Christ. Anything you say is just an opinion. Anything he says is law. Deliver his message with complete confidence.

Be Yourself

Authenticity means that you simply be yourself. People have built-in imposter detectors. They can spot a fake a mile away.

People want to know: Do you really care about them? Do you really have an authentic relationship with Jesus? Do you really practice what you preach? Are you the same person on stage that you are off stage?

Charles Spurgeon said, "The life of the preacher should be a magnet to draw men to Christ, and it is sad indeed when it keeps them from him."[9] If you are not authentic in your faith and preaching, you will repel people from Christ like the same sides of a magnet.

So if your preaching is not an authentic expression of your walk with God, then please stop preaching. Like I said at the beginning of this book, you have

---

[9]   Spurgeon, *Lectures*, 18.

to work out of an authentic relationship with God first.

Authenticity is one of the foundational pillars of preaching. It doesn't matter how polished your speaking ability is; if you aren't authentic, people won't listen. *Who* you are is as important as *what* you say and *how* you say it. And in today's culture of many fakes, there is little more attractive than real authenticity.

Listen to how Paul describes his preaching: "When I came to you, I did not come with eloquence or human wisdom as I proclaimed to you the testimony about God. For I resolved to know nothing while I was with you except Jesus Christ and him crucified. I came to you in weakness with great fear and trembling. My message and my preaching were not with wise and persuasive words, but with a demonstration of the Spirit's power, so that your faith might not rest on human wisdom, but on God's power." (1 Corinthians 2:1-5 NIV).

What could be more authentic than that? The power of Paul's preaching was not in his words. Paul preached in weakness, fear, and trembling. The power was in his authentic love for Christ and the power of God working through him. May your preaching be the same.

ACTION STEP: Look in the Mirror

Take a hard look at yourself in the mirror. Are you authentic? Is there anything in your life that has the potential to destroy your credibility and authenticity as a preacher?

We all have things in our life that God is working on as we walk through the life-long process of sanctification. But the key is to identify them, so we can seek God's help to overcome the power of this sin in our lives.

Identify one thing in your life that you need to change. Maybe it's a form of pride, lust, greed, envy, bitterness, laziness, or dwindling spiritual life.

Once you have identified your one thing, pray about it. Beg God to help you overcome this problem. Now, take radical action to do whatever God convicts you to do about it. You may need to confess, repent, and seek accountability or counseling.

2. GESTURES: Speak With Your Body

We walk around all day waving our arms and making extensive use of our hands as we communicate to everyone around us. But when we step up to speak it's as though the arms are hollow and someone has poured them full of cement. Or in front of an audience we repeat one gesture over and over like a robot with a short circuit. Nervous tension and habit are the culprits.

— Ken Davis[10]

---

[10]   Ken Davis, *Secrets of Dynamic Communications: Prepare with Focus, Deliver with Clarity, Speak with Power* (Nashville: Thomas Nelson, 2013), 100.

When I was a kid, my parents threw together spontaneous game nights with my three brothers and me. We played a lot of different games, but one of our favorites was Simon Says.

If you've ever played before, you know the rules. One person is "it." They stand in front of everyone and give commands. Everyone has to do what they say if they begin the command with "Simon says."

So they might touch their elbow and say "Simon says touch your elbow." So you touch your elbow. Then, they might jump in the air shouting, "Jump in the air!" If you jump, you are out, because they didn't say "Simon Says."

Dad would usually be "it" first, and my brothers and I would compete to see who could last the longest. I was pretty good. I trained my ear to only allow my body to move when I heard "Simon says." But there was one trick that always got me.

My dad would say something like "Simon says touch your nose." But he touched his ear. I copied my dad and touched my ear, but my older brother, Blake, touched his nose. Blake won, and I collapsed in defeat because I followed what my dad did, not what he said.

Preaching is kind of like Simon Says. The goal in preaching is to communicate a clear message. And we speak with more than words. We also speak with our bodies.

Many studies have shown that a large part of communication is nonverbal. Factors such as posture, gestures, and facial expressions play a role in how someone interprets what we say. Some studies even suggest that nonverbal communication overpowers verbal communication. So when a speaker's words and body language don't align, the audience will hear the body more than the words.

Like Simon Says, when you direct the audience to do something, they will copy your body movement more than your words. Actions really do speak louder than words.

Every movement of the body communicates something whether you are aware of it or not. Christian comedian and speaker Ken Davis says, "There is no such thing as a neutral gesture. Everything you do with your hands communicates something. Make sure your hands are not giving a speech in competition with the one you are delivering."[11] So we must know what our movements say and gain control of them to ensure they're not conflicting our message.

---

[11]   Davis, *Dynamic Communications*, 101.

Like it or not, preaching is far more than just your words. So the best preachers don't just preach with their lips, but with their entire body.

There are four areas of body language that we will discuss in this chapter: posture, gestures, movement, and facial expressions.

Posture

What is your natural stance on stage? How should you stand?

There may be nothing more unnatural-feeling than standing naturally in front of a crowd. It sounds funny, but it's true. So you need to work on your resting stance—your default stance between gestures.

The best stance is to have good posture with your back straight, chest out, head up, arms relaxed at sides, and feet shoulder-width apart. It communicates that you are confident but also relaxed. You may feel awkward at first, but it looks natural.

Good posture also keeps your airways open so your lungs have the capacity to power your voice. If you preach multiple services or for more than 30 minutes, you need your lungs to work for you. For this reason, Charles Spurgeon taught aspiring preachers, "Do not speak with your hands in your waistcoat pockets so as to contract your lungs, but throw the shoulders back as public singers do. Do not lean over a desk while speaking, and never hold the head down on the breast while preaching. Upward rather than downward let the body bend."[12]

Unfortunately, I have seen many pastors with bad posture. Your posture is a form of nonverbal communication. Whether you intend to or not, you always communicate something with your posture.

Think about how people might interpret someone standing in various ways:

- **Too stiff**: When a person stands like a robot (back, neck, and joints stiff), they communicate that they are uptight, uncomfortable, nervous, or dull.

- **Slouching**: A person who is slouching (head and shoulders down) communicates that they are nervous, insecure, ashamed, or bored.

- **Hands on hips**: When someone puts both hands on their hips they convey a sense of pride, arrogance, or speaking down to the audience.

---

[12] Charles H. Spurgeon, *Lectures To My Students* (Fig, 2012), 123.

- **Crossed arms**: Crossing your arms can be a sign of defensiveness—like you are trying to protect yourself. People may perceive you as disengaged, hostile, or in disagreement with something.

- **Hands clasped**: When a speaker holds their hands together, it gives a sense of weakness, nervousness, or even wanting protection—like a basketball player setting a screen on a defender.

- **Hands in pockets**: Although putting your hand in your pocket can feel relaxed, people see it as a sign that you are nervous, or distracted. It also distracts people who will wonder what's in your pocket.

Avoid all these in your resting stance, but please don't misunderstand me. I'm not saying you can never use these postures. In fact, you may want to use some of them, like crossed arms or hands on hips as gestures to animate your message. But as a resting stance, avoid these.

Although it may not feel natural at first, practice a resting stance with good posture: back straight, chest out, head up, arms relaxed at sides, and feet shoulder width apart.

Gestures

What should you do with your body while preaching? If you stand too stiff, you will be boring. You need to gesture—move your body in a way that compliments what you are saying.

As Bryan Chapell observes, "In a lively conversation, our hands naturally come up so that they are within the line of sight of the people we address. When our hands do less in the pulpit, we appear awkward and uncomfortable."[13]

The best advice I have heard about gestures is to not think about them. Why? The best gestures are natural. They flow out of the content of your message. If you plan all your gestures, they can feel rehearsed.

Think about the last time you sat around the dinner table with old friends telling stories. You relaxed. Your hands flowed with the conversation. When the story got exciting, your hands moved faster. When it was calm, your hands moved slower. When you talked about the shape of something, you formed it with

---

[13] Bryan Chapell, *Christ-Centered Preaching: Redeeming the Expository Sermon*, Kindle ed. (Grand Rapids: Baker, 2015), Location 7547.

your hands. When you spoke about an action, your hands (maybe your whole body) performed the action.

That's how gestures in your preaching should be, natural, like a great conversation among the best of friends. But most people are not naturals at gestures on stage. Nerves and overthinking get in the way.

Here are some general rules on good times to use gestures:

- **Number**: Use gestures to aid the communicate numbers or order. For example, If you say, "There were three of us," hold up three fingers. If you are listing your points and say, "Second," hold up two fingers.

- **Position**: Use gestures to communicate the direction or position of something. For example, if you say, "One day we will be up in Heaven," raise your hand and point up. Or if you say, "Sitting to his right," motion both hands to the right.

- **Shape**: Use gestures to draw shapes. For example, if you say, "She was very pregnant," move your hands around your imaginary pregnant belly. Motion your hands in a circle when you

31

say, "The whole Earth." If you say, "They delivered a large box," move your hands to form the sides of an invisible square.

- **Movement**: Use gestures to show movement. For example, if you say, "He threw the football," make a football throwing motion. If you say, "The river flowed," make waves with your hand. "She ducked just in time!" Duck.

- **Emotion**: Use gestures to help express emotions. For instance, if you say, "I was furious," furl your brow and shake your fists. Make a sad face and motion tears from your eyes if you say, "She cried." Or if you say, "He felt defeated," drop your hands to your side and slump your head and shoulders.

Natural gestures that complement a message elevate a preacher's excitement, engagement, and effectiveness. Bad gestures, like holding up one finger when you say, "three," distract from the message and confuse your audience.

So get in the habit of communicating with gestures. Work on it in your sermons, and practice in your daily conversations. But don't go overboard, or force it.

If you are a naturally expressive person in conversation, that's great. If you are naturally more subdued, that's OK. Use gestures consistent with your personality.

Movement

Movement is different from gestures. By gestures, I'm referring to the way you communicate with your body (often with your hands). By movement, I mean moving from one location of the room to another (with your feet).

Like gestures, movement can either engage or distract your audience. For example, when I was a teenager, the youth pastor at my church was a pacer. He took three steps to the left, paused, three steps to the right, paused, and back again. He looked like a caged tiger at the zoo.

To this day I can't remember a lot of what he said, but I remember his pacing clear as day. Distracting movements rob your sermon of its power.

Movement varies among pastors. Some plant their feet behind a pulpit and never move. Others run up and down the aisles. Most are somewhere in between.

Too much movement is distracting, but zero movement is dull. You have to find a balance of what works best for your personality and your audience. However you move while preaching, make sure it is for a reason.

Use movement to:

- **Communicate excitement:** Dead things don't move; living things do. The more you move, the more alive and passionate you will appear.

- **Grab attention:** Moving things get our attention. It's why we keep glancing at the TV in the restaurant when we should focus on our date instead.

- **Demonstrate a point:** If movement can illustrate a point in your sermon, do it.

- **Act a story:** If you are telling a story with some action, it can be helpful if you move a bit to act it out.

- **Transition between points:** Movement can be useful for signaling a shift to a new point. For example, you could stand to the left for your first point, move to the right for you second, and center for your last point.

There are many ways that movement can cause distractions. Here are a few things to be cautious about:

- **Pacing:** Pacing is distracting. It signals that you are nervous. Plus, it's uncomfortable. Try pacing during your next conversation in the office and watch people's reactions. Pacing makes people nervous. Move to one side of the stage and hang out for a while. What's the rush?

- **Frantic steps:** You need to control your movement. Don't get carried away. This is especially true if you are recording the sermon video for multiple campuses or online viewers because the camera person will have a hard time keeping you in the frame. Also, rapid camera movement makes some people motion sick. Please don't nauseate people with your preaching.

- **Lights:** If you preach in a dark room, avoid moving to areas of the stage that are not well lit, or your audience won't be able to see you. Younger listeners may not have trouble, but older eyes can't see as well in dim lighting.

- **Speakers:** Be careful moving in front of any speakers with a microphone. Getting too close to a speaker can cause deafening feedback.

As much as movement can be an aid to communication, it can also be a huge distraction. So either move with purpose or don't move at all.

Facial Expressions

Like gestures, your facial expressions should be natural. They should match the tone of what you are saying. Your face should connect with the mood.

For many preachers, a serious expression comes easy. We have no problem talking about serious matters of God with a cold stare and a furrowed brow. But we can be so serious that we forget to smile. When you speak of joy in Christ with a frown, you send the wrong signal.

Your tone should match your face. According to Bryan Chapell, "If you can smile in the pulpit, you can convey every other needed expression... It is practically impossible not to smile and sound joyful or to sound sincere and not furrow your brow."[14]

---

14   Chapell, *Christ-Centered Preaching*, Location 7521.

You have to learn to relax your face to express the right tone. Smile when it's joyful. Lower your eyebrows when it's solemn. Widen your eyes when it's surprising.

Overall, facial expressions are best when you don't need to think about it because it's simply a natural reaction to the tone of your message.

What Does Your Body Preach?

Like it or not, your body speaks. Every movement communicates something.

Yes, there are more important elements of preaching like the way you interpret a text, pray, or follow the inspiration of the Holy Spirit. But non-verbal communication is still a huge part of communication.

You need to find balance and purpose in your movement. Too much movement is a distraction; too little is a bore.

The biggest enemies of your body are the nervous ticks and habits that conflict your message, lessen your effectiveness, and distract the listener. All preachers have them. You need to fight them.

Ask yourself: What body movements do you have when you preach? Maybe you have a nervous tick that you do with your hands. Maybe you pace while you preach. Maybe you have bad posture. Almost everyone has something they have to focus on eliminating. Even the best, most experienced preachers can still slide into bad habits.

Whatever it is, repetitive movements and gestures that don't connect with what you are saying reveal your nerves, and worse, distract your audience.

If your gestures and words do not align, your preaching is like a game of Simon Says where everyone loses. So loosen up.

ACTION STEP: Mute Your Video

Record and watch a video of yourself preaching, but mute the sound. Without being able to hear the words, evaluate what you are communicating with your body.

What are your postures, gestures, movements, and facial expressions telling the audience? Does it align with your message? Identify any distracting habits that you need to eliminate, and keep a tally of how many times you do it in the sermon.

Repeat this practice every week with a goal to lower the number of times you do it each week until you are free from your bad habit.

3. EYES: Look At People

The eyes can spit fire, pour out compassion, and preach Christ in you. When you deny people your eyes, you really deny them yourself.

— *Bryan Chapell*[15]

I love visiting churches. I step onto church property for the first time, pretending I know nothing about church. It provides tremendous insight into how people might feel when they come to visit my church for the first time.

Recently, I visited a new church that I had never attended. They had a nice building. Their volunteers

---

[15]   Bryan Chapell, *Christ-Centered Preaching: Redeeming the Expository Sermon*, Kindle ed. (Grand Rapids: Baker, 2015), Location 7512.

were friendly. The music was good. But as I sat and listened to the pastor, for some reason I was having trouble connecting.

The content was good, but something in his delivery was off. That's when I realized the problem. The pastor had lousy eye contact.

His eyes bounced left, right, then down at his notes.

Left. Right. Notes.

Left. Right. Notes.

Left. Right. Notes.

He reminded me of one of those old cat clocks where the eyes move back and forth every second. Although he built the message well, his eyes betrayed him. His nerves showed. And it made it hard to watch and listen. Don't let your eyes betray a good sermon.

The Four Benefits of Eye Contact

Eye contact is critical for four major reasons: trust, confidence, engagement, and awareness. Let me explain.

1. Trust

When someone lies to you, what do their eyes do? They look away. Unless they are a fantastic liar, they won't look you in the eyes, because they are ashamed of the lie. That is why people will say, "Look me in the eyes and tell me the truth." It's also why professional poker players wear sunglasses. It's hard to lie while holding eye contact.

"A speaker who will not look people in the eyes is deemed aloof, afraid, and/ or incompetent," says Bryan Chapell. "One who looks at the ceiling while explaining how Jesus held little children appears distracted. One who looks at the floor while exhorting others to repent seems intimidated. One who looks over heads (or even at foreheads) instead of in the eyes of listeners seems untrustworthy."[16]

The point is: when you preach with poor eye contact, people will be less likely to trust you. It naturally communicates deceit. If you don't hold eye contact when making bold claims, people will question your sincerity. The power of your preaching will suffer.

Now, I know you are not lying. You genuinely believe what you are saying. But if you aren't careful, your eyes will sabotage you.

People are more likely to trust you when you look them in the eyes. You have to hold eye contact with

---

[16]   Chapell, *Christ-Centered Preaching*, Location 7508.

individual people in the room for more than a few seconds at a time.

Steady eye contact builds trust and improves communication.

2. Confidence

Nerves are the main reason people don't look their audience in the eyes. You are afraid of their reactions. So your eyes bounce from the carpet to the ceiling to the back wall, but not to people's eyes.

The other reason you may not look people in the eyes is if you don't know the material well enough. You look at your notes constantly. Either you are not prepared enough, or your notes are like a security blanket. You may not need them, but you keep looking at them for comfort. (We will discuss notes more in Chapter 13).

Both of these cases are a lack of confidence either in yourself or the message.

Strong eye contact is a sign of confidence. Think about the most insecure person you have ever met. They rarely make eye contact with you or anyone in a room. Now think about the most confident person you know. They look you straight in the eyes, don't they?

Eye contact is a natural sign of confidence. When you look your audience in the eye, you show them that you believe in the value of what you are saying. You are confident in the message. You are a person worth listening to.

Calvin Miller, in his book *Preaching: The Art of Narrative Exposition*, points out that "'eye contact' means exactly what it says: the eye of the speaker meets the eye of the listeners... If you feel insecure looking into people's eyes, get over it!"[17]

If you struggle with nerves, you have to push through that. If your notes are a problem, you have to get rid of them. Get to the root of your lack of confidence, and trust in God.

You may be putting way too much stock in yourself. Be confident in the message God has given you. Take hold of God's promise that His Word "will not return to me empty, but will accomplish what I desire and achieve the purpose for which I sent it" (Isaiah 55:11 NIV).

3. Engagement

Imagine you are driving your car. You stop at a red light, and do what many of us do—no, I'm not

---

17   Calvin Miller, *Preaching: The Art of Narrative Exposition* (Grand Rapids: Baker, 2006), 196.

talking about the epidemic of looking at your phone until you almost miss the green light. You look at the person in the car next to you. And what do they do? They look right back at you. So you quickly look away and pretend you were looking at something else.

Why does this happen? It's like we can almost sense when other people are looking at us. However it works, it gets our attention. When you look at someone, they look at you. They are instantly engaged with you, whether you like it or not.

I learned this principle of eye contact from preaching to middle school students. It's hard to find a more distracted audience than a room filled with over a hundred 13-year-olds. I'm a firm believer that the more middle schoolers you put in a room, the lower their collective IQ and attention span get. I had to learn how to keep them engaged, or my message was lost.

Sometimes you have no choice but to call them out when they are talking too much or hitting the person next to them. "Hey Jimmy, I can hear you from way up here, bro. Shh."

But many times, all it takes is a look. So if I notice a group of girls talking, I simply continue preaching while looking straight at them. It doesn't take long before one of them looks up and sees me staring their direction. They suddenly snap to attention and look at me. Why? Because they know I am looking at them.

Your eyes are a powerful tool. When you look at people, they look at you. It makes the message personal. You aren't just speaking into the abyss; you are speaking to them.

Haddon Robinson, in his book *Biblical Preaching*, says it this way: "When you look listeners in the eye, they feel that you want to talk with them personally. Therefore, pastors who gaze over their audiences' heads, read a manuscript, stare down at notes, look out of windows, or worse, shut their eyes while they speak, place themselves at a crippling disadvantage."[18]

4. Awareness

The final benefit of eye contact is awareness. When you look at the people in the room instead of your notes or the back wall, you have the critical ability to read them.

When you look at your audience, you can see if you have connected or if they look confused. You will know if you are losing people or if they are leaning in.

---

[18]   Haddon W. Robinson, *Biblical Preaching: The Development and Delivery of Expository Messages* (Grand Rapids: Baker, 2001) 212.

You will see if people smile at your joke or if it bombs. You will see if people are taking notes, nodding their heads, or resting their eyes for a little siesta.

Monitoring the pulse of your audience while you are preaching allows you to react in the moment. If a joke gets no reaction, you can laugh about how bad that was and regain your audience. If people look confused, you can explain what you said again from a better angle.

Audience awareness helps you get real-time feedback from your message. You will know what connects, what doesn't, and when you need to adjust your message. Overall, you will be a far better preacher if you read your audience while you speak.

Work On It

The primary rule for eye contact is counterintuitive: When you look at everyone, you connect with no one. But when you focus on one, you connect with everyone.

Good eye contact while preaching is not a natural tendency; it's a learned habit. You have to be intentional about it. You have to practice.

The next time you preach, try this: look left, right, and middle. Lock eyes with a person on the left side of the room. Hold it for ten seconds or so. Take your time and make your point. Then, look a person in the eyes on the right side of the room. Hold for a moment. Then, work back to the middle of the room, and hold it. Repeat until it becomes natural.

In the back of your mind, you have to be thinking, "eye contact, eye contact, eye contact." You may even need to write it in large letters at the top of your notes.

It might be easier for you if you walk the stage. Walk to the left, talk to the people over there for a while. Walk to the right, speak to those people for a while. Then, come back to the center. Just remember to be slow and take your time. If you move too fast, you will look like a hyperactive kid after a shot of espresso.

However you do it, you have to think about eye contact until it becomes natural. At first, it will be awkward. You will notice things you never noticed before. You may see people who are disengaged and disinterested. You will have to fight getting distracted.

If you are preaching to a tough crowd, lock eyes with the people who are most engaged—the guy leaning forward to hear every word or the lady nodding her head in agreement. These people will encourage you to keep preaching until the others get on board.

Eye contact is a vital element of good communication. Do it well, and you will engage people.

ACTION STEP: Awkward Eyes

Do this experiment: The next conversation you have, stare at the floor the whole time or dart your eyes all around the room. Just don't look the other person in the eyes for more than one second at a time. See how the conversation goes.

Write about your experience in a notebook or journal. How did it feel? How did the other person react?

Then, in your very next conversation, lock on to their eyes with yours. Even if it is a little uncomfortable, keep looking them in the eyes. Don't allow your gaze to drift.

Write about your experience this time. What was the difference?

Practice locking eyes with individuals in your audience in the same way. Hold your gaze with theirs while you deliver your point, then move to another person for your next point.

If you need a reminder, write **"EYE CONTACT"** at the top of your notes.

4. VOICE: Vary Your Voice

Vary your voice continually. Vary your speed as well—dash as rapidly as a lightning flash, and anon, travel forward in quiet majesty. Shift your accent, move your emphasis, and avoid sing-song. Vary the tone; use the bass sometimes, and let the thunders roll within; at other times speak as you ought to do generally—from the lips, and let your speech be conversational... Human nature craves for variety, and God grants it in nature, providence and grace; let us have it in sermons also.

— Charles Spurgeon[19]

---

[19]   Charles H. Spurgeon, *Lectures To My Students* (Fig, 2012), 132.

You step on stage. The lights come up. Everyone is looking at you.

Adrenaline starts pumping as your fight or flight response kicks in. You are nervous.

Here's the problem: the nerves and adrenaline rush that are common in public speaking cause most pastors to preach too fast.

If you are too excited or too nervous, you get the same result. You rush through your sermon. When excited, you rush to get to the next point. When nervous, you rush to get it over.

If you speak too fast, your audience may have trouble keeping up with you. They won't be able to think about the words you say, and your message will lose impact.

Although it's less common, some preachers can also speak too slow. Slow preachers appear apathetic. Their audience may also become bored and wish you would hurry up and say it already. People may begin thinking about other things, and your message will lose impact.

When was the last time you evaluated the pace of your preaching? How would you grade yourself?

If you want to become a better preacher, you have to master your speaking pace. But what is the perfect pace? Faster? Slower? Somewhere in between?

The answer is "Yes." You need all three. You need to have variety in your sermon. If you preach at the same pace for the entire sermon, your audience will lose focus. Your speaking will become white noise, no matter how fast or slow it is.

Have you ever noticed that prescription drug commercials do this on purpose? At the end of the commercial, the narrator reads the list of possible side effects without any change of pace. While you look at images of people smiling, doing fun activities, or sitting outdoors in separate bathtubs (who does that?), the narrator is droning on about all the ways this drug could give you diarrhea, high blood pressure, heart attacks, hearing loss, or flat-out kill you. Yikes!

But unless you focus hard on the words, you will tune out the narrator's disclaimer because the pace is unvaried. And that is exactly what pharmaceutical companies hope you do. They want you to focus on the happy people, not the terrifying disclaimer they're required by law to include.

Here's the point: If you don't vary your pace, people will tune you out like a drug commercial. You need to mix it up.

We worship the God of variety. When creating the universe, He could have created only one kind of fruit and called it a day. Instead, He created countless varieties of fruit. He could have created people to all look the same. Instead, He created each of us to be wonderfully diverse. The world is such a fascinating place to explore because there is so much variety.

Variety grips our interest. Sameness, like the sound of a babbling brook, lulls us to sleep.

To master the art of preaching, you must have variety in the pace that words flow from your mouth. You must learn when to vary the pace of your speech using all three speeds.

1. Average pace – conversation

To start, you need to nail down your average speaking pace. This is your baseline. It's the pace that the majority of your message should default to, and the standard by which you will either speed up or slow down.

Your average pace should be neither too fast nor too slow. If it's too fast, speeding up will sound like an auctioneer rifling through words. If it's too slow, slowing down will sound like someone shot you with a tranquilizer dart.

It may be best to think of your average pace being close to your normal conversational speed. If you were having a one-on-one conversation with a good friend over lunch, how fast would you talk? I'm not talking about when you are excited and naturally increase your pace of speech; I mean your speed in a normal conversation.

According to Andy Stanley, in his book *Communicating for a Change*, an engaging speaker's average pace should be slightly above their normal conversational speed. If you want to get technical, the average pace for English speakers is 150 words per minute. A faster speaker may reach 190 words per minutes.[20] A slower speaker may hover around 130.

If you tend to be a fast talker, like me, you will need to force yourself to slow down to achieve your best average pace.

2. Fast pace – excitement

Use a more rapid rate of speech to communicate urgency, excitement, or passion.

---

[20]   Andy Stanley, *Communicating for a Change: Seven Keys to Irresistible Communication* (Colorado Springs: Multnomah, 2006), 156.

Speeding up is like putting an exclamation point on a sentence. It lets the audience know you are excited!

A fast pace is good for:

- Telling an exciting part of a story.

- Expressing enthusiasm about an idea or upcoming event.

- Getting your audience excited.

- Setting up the audience right before slowing down to emphasize a big idea or deliver a punch line.

In daily conversations, when you are excited or angry, your pace and volume increase. You speak louder and faster. And the tone of your voice changes.

Your fast pace should be like this—not necessarily shouting at people, but clearly expressing the excitement, urgency, or righteous anger in your voice.

3. Slow pace – emphasis

Using a slower rate of speech communicates seriousness and significance. When you go fast and suddenly slow, it signals to the audience, "Listen! This is important."

Slowing down is like putting a word in your sentence in **bold** or *italics*. It's a variation from the norm that highlights an important word or phrase to your audience.

A slow pace is good for:

- Giving complicated thoughts time to sink in.

- Explaining terminology the audience may be unfamiliar with.

- Emphasizing a major point that you do not want people to miss.

- Talking about serious things such as death, suffering, or consequences of sin.

- Reading a profound passage of Scripture or a quote.

The key is knowing when to speak at an average pace, when to speed up, or when to slow down. This only comes with practice.

More Pacing Factors:

Concerning your pace and vocal variety, there are a few other things you should consider.

Say less

I'm often guilty of speaking too fast because I have more to say than time to say it. I want to cram it all in, so I speed up to say everything before time runs out. I set myself up to fail before I speak a word because I wrote too much and cut too little.

A sermon is not a race against the clock. You will never be able to say everything about any topic in just one message. The Bible is a collection of God's revealed truth to us over thousands of years. Jesus spent three years teaching all the lessons recorded in the Gospels. There are instances where we see that Jesus taught until "the day began to wear away" (Luke 9:12, ESV). So what makes us think we could say everything in 30-minutes?

You are not supposed to say it all. So stop trying. Slow down and say a few things well.

Learn how much content you can preach in your allotted sermon time. Look over your message. Keep only the best content. Focus on one key point and save the rest for another sermon.

If you catch yourself running out of time to say everything you planned to say, remember this: Nobody else knows what you wanted to say. You may get upset that you didn't get to a point, but unless you leave a section blank on an outline you handed out, your audience will never know. It's OK to edit your sermon on the fly instead of trying to speed up or preach too long to fit it all in.

Enunciate

One of the pitfalls of fast preaching is poor enunciation—not pronouncing words clearly. You may think people understood you because you know the words you meant to say. But what the audience hears could be completely different.

For example, in the debates leading up to the 2016 Presidential Election in the United States, Donald Trump repeatedly said the phrase, "big league," but he didn't enunciate. Many people thought he said, "bigly." So Google searches began to spike for the word "bigly," and people mocked Trump for making up a word and having poor grammar. Merriam-Webster even named "bigly" as one of the top words of 2016 because so many people searched for its definition.[21]

Even though Trump apparently meant to say "big league," it doesn't matter. His failure to enunciate became an unnecessary distraction.

---

[21]   "Gallery: Word of the Year 2016." Cited 7 January 2017. Online: https://www.merriam-webster.com/ words-at-play/word-of-the-year-2016/bigly

Communication is not just what you think you say; it's what the audience hears. If you intend to say one thing, but the audience hears something different, what did you communicate?

Don't rush words. You will sound mumbled, as your words blend together. Slow your pace and pronounce words clearly.

Watch your tone

The tone of your voice affects your pace and determines how people interpret the message.

For example, consider the sentence "I hate you." It's a strong phrase, but I hear it in different contexts. Sometimes people shout it with malice in their voice as an insult. But I often hear it said playfully. With this tone, it's friendly banter or even flirting.

The tone of your voice should match the mood of your message. If the words are meant to be joyful, your voice should be happy. If the words are intended to be fiery, your voice should be intense. Otherwise, if the tone doesn't fit the mood, it can be inappropriate. For example, you should not speak of human suffering with a cheerful tone.

Tim Keller says it well in his book *Preaching*: "It is far more effective when a speaker can move from sweetness and sunshine to clouds and thunder! Let the biblical text control you, not your temperament. Learn to communicate 'loud' truth as loud; 'hard' truth as hard; and 'sweet' truth as sweet. "[22]

Pause

Think of pauses as punctuation marks. If there is a comma in a sentence, it should signal a short pause. A period, question mark, or exclamation point should signal a full pause.

We will discuss pauses further in the next chapter. For now, just know that they relate to your speaking pace, and are another tool in your arsenal of vocal variety.

How to Practice Your Pace

At the end of this chapter, I will give you one action step to help you work on your preaching pace, but there is more than one way to improve.

Here are a few suggestions to try:

Practice while reading

Read a book or article out loud like it's a sermon. Read at your average speed. Practice speeding up and

---

[22] Timothy Keller, *Preaching: Communicating Faith in an Age of Skepticism*, Kindle ed. (New York: Penguin, 2015), 160.

slowing down at various parts for excitement or emphasis. Pause at punctuation marks.

I love reading bedtime stories to my kids. If you have young children (or grandchildren, nieces, or nephews), read them a story while also practicing your pace. It makes the story more entertaining for the kids, and you get practice. Everybody wins.

Practice while rehearsing

When you rehearse your sermon before preaching (as you should), work on your average pace and find the parts where you should speed up or slow down.

Make a mental note, or consider marking in your notes where you want to preach fast or slow. Consider doing things like making important points you want to emphasize **bold** or *italicized*. It could be an indicator for you to slow down and deliver it with clarity and power.

Practice with your favorite preacher

Did you ever play the copy game when you were a kid—where someone talks, and you repeat everything they say? You may have been annoying, but now you can put those skills to good use!

So you don't look crazy, find a place you can be alone. Play a sermon podcast from your favorite preacher, and repeat what they say out loud. You will soon get a feel for their pace, and probably one of the many reasons you enjoy listening to them.

The better feel you get for a good preaching pace, the easier it will be for you to replicate it on stage.

Note: Your goal should not be to become a copy of your favorite preacher. You need to be who God created you to be. The goal is to learn from them, not become them.

Practice watching good movies

Great actors are great orators. They have mastered varying their speaking pace depending on the mood of the scene.

Watch your favorite movie from a new perspective, focusing on the pace of speech. Casual conversations will be different than an inspirational speech, romantic moment, or an action-packed event.

See what you can learn. How might this translate to your preaching?

Vary Your Voice

There is a huge difference between words heard and ideas understood. If you speak too fast, your audience may hear all your words, but their brains may not be able to keep up to understand all your ideas. If you speak too slow, their minds will think much faster than you speak, and their thoughts will move ahead to other matters.

Never stop evaluating the pace of your preaching. Even if you have been preaching for a long time, it's easy to fall back into old habits.

There... is... nothing... more... boring... than... a... plodding... preacher. Please, don't be that pastor!

Speak at a solid pace, then slow down or speed up for emphasis. Don't be afraid to raise your voice for excitement, make sound effects when telling a story, or whisper in a tender moment. Moving your voice, like moving your body, captures attention.

People need space to think, and variety to keep their attention. A great message wrapped in a monotone voice is a tragedy.

I love how Charles Spurgeon taught this to his students:

"What a pity that a man who from his heart delivered doctrines of undoubted value, in language the most appropriate, should commit ministerial suicide by harping on one string, when the Lord had given him an instrument of many strings to play upon! Alas! alas! for that dreary voice, it hummed and hummed like a

mill-wheel to the same unmusical turn, whether its owner spake of heaven or hell, eternal life or everlasting wrath. It might be, by accident, a little louder or softer, according to the length of the sentence, but its tone was still the same, a dreary waste of sound, a howling wilderness of speech in which there was no possible relief, no variety, no music, nothing but horrible sameness."[23]

ACTION STEP: *Study Your Pace*

Record your next sermon, or use an old recording, and evaluate your pace. Have a copy of your notes with you. Follow along with the sermon and mark you notes at parts that could have benefitted by speaking slower or faster.

Now, answer these questions:

- Is your average speaking pace too fast, too slow, or just right?

- What parts of your sermon do you tend to speak too fast?

---

[23]   Spurgeon, *Lectures*, 111.

- Where parts of your sermon do you tend to speak too slow?

- What major point of your sermon would you have benefitted from speaking slowly for greater emphasis?

- How was your pace when reading Scripture?

- Did your tone match the mood of the message?

- Who will you ask to help keep you accountable and help evaluate the pace of your next sermon, so you continue to improve?

5. PAUSE: Punctuate Your Sentences

By your silence you shall speak.

— *Rudyard Kipling*[24]

One of the biggest mistakes that preachers make is neglecting the power of the pause.

Many of us are afraid of silence. We think we have to fill every second with words. Silence is awkward. We are tempted to run from it and speed through our message as fast as possible.

As a result, where a pause should be, we add filler words like "umm..." and "uhh..." In doing so, we miss

---

[24]   Rudyard Kipling as quoted in Haddon W. Robinson, *Biblical Preaching: The Development and Delivery of Expository Messages* (Grand Rapids: Baker, 2001) 217.

out on one of the most powerful tools in a preacher's toolkit—the pause.

Bryan Chapell says it well: "The best speakers not only vary their expression from thundering to whispering and their pace from crawling to racing but also let their most telling statements echo in pauses that emphasize thought."[25]

The best preachers know when to pause, because silence is the punctuation of a sermon.

A Story Without Punctuation

Imagine reading a novel with no punctuation marks or paragraph breaks. Would you enjoy it? Would it stir your imagination?

Try this: Read the following quote out loud. It's one of my favorites from C.S. Lewis' classic *The Lion, the Witch, and the Wardrobe*, except all punctuation has been removed.

> *Aslan a man said Mr Beaver sternly Certainly not I tell you he is King of the wood and the son of the great emperor beyond the sea Dont you know who is the King of the Beasts Aslan is a lion the Lion the great lion ooh said Susan Id*

---

25   Bryan Chapell, *Christ-Centered Preaching: Redeeming the Expository Sermon*, Kindle ed. (Grand Rapids: Baker, 2015), Location 7487.

thought he was a man Is he quite safe I shall feel rather nervous about meeting a lion That you will dearie and no mistake said Mrs Beaver if theres anyone who can appear before Aslan without their knees knocking theyre either braver than most or else just silly Then he isnt safe said Lucy Safe said Mr Beaver don't you hear what Mrs Beaver tells you Who said anything about safe Course he isnt safe But hes good

This is what a sermon without pauses sounds like. Rushed. Cluttered. No space to breathe.

Now, read it again with punctuation. Make sure to pause at every period, comma, question mark, and exclamation point.

"Aslan a man!" said Mr. Beaver sternly. "Certainly not. I tell you he is King of the wood and the son of the great Emperor-beyond-the-Sea. Don't you know who is the King of the Beasts? Aslan is a lion—the Lion, the great Lion."

"Ooh!" said Susan, "I'd thought he was a man. Is he—quite safe? I shall feel rather nervous about meeting a lion."

"That you will, dearie, and no mistake," said Mrs. Beaver; "if there's anyone who can appear before Aslan without their knees knocking, they're either braver than most or else just silly."

"Then he isn't safe?" said Lucy.

"Safe?" said Mr. Beaver; "don't you hear what Mrs. Beaver tells you? Who said anything about safe? 'Course he isn't safe. But he's good."[26]

The difference is obvious—even for the 90 percent of you who didn't read out loud like I asked.

A good sermon should speed up, slow down, and pause in the same way a writer intends words to flow from the page. Pause before a key word to set it apart, and after a powerful idea to let it sink in.

Pauses are the punctuation marks of sermons. Sometimes you need commas—brief pauses. Sometimes you need periods—full stops. And sometimes you need ellipses—long breaks for suspense.

Pauses are the white space on the page that gives your words contrast, meaning, and room to breathe. They give people time to think. They allow the listen-

---

[26] C.S. Lewis, *The Lion, the Witch and the Wardrobe* (New York: Harper Collins, 2005), 80-81.

er's brain time to process and digest the propositions you are asking them to believe.

If you know you have a good line or a powerful statement, pause for a moment before and after the delivery. Allow the audience to savor that sentence.

Now, I am convinced that pastors enter a distortion of the space-time continuum while preaching, because a pause while preaching feels like an eternity. Have you experienced this phenomenon? It's uncomfortable. All that time, everyone looking at you, and no words. But from the audience's perspective, a pause that feels long to you feels right.

You have to learn to embrace the awkwardness of silence. Because in reality, it isn't awkward at all. What's awkward is a preacher who never stops to take a breath.

Silence is your friend, not the enemy. Don't let it scare you. Embrace it.

5 Ways Pauses Benefit Your Preaching

Although it may be clear to you now that pauses are essential to good preaching, how exactly do help?

There are five major ways that mastering the pause will benefit your sermon:

1. It gives the preacher time to concentrate before thoughtful delivery.

2. It allows the audience time to gather their thoughts and prepare to receive your message.

3. It builds suspense and anticipation.

4. It highlights an important idea, giving it time to sink in.

5. It shows command of your message.

As Charles Spurgeon says: "Know how to pause. Make a point of interjecting arousing parentheses of quietude. Speech is silver, but silence is golden."[27]

So practice pauses to help vary your speaking. Practice pausing at punctuation when reading your message out loud.

Consider pausing before and after a phrase to create emphasis. Pause to build anticipation for what you are going to say next. Pause before the punchline of a joke to increase its power. Pause when your audience responds in laughter or applause.

Obviously, too much silence can also be a bad thing. So I suggest keeping pause up to five seconds

---

[27] Charles H. Spurgeon, *Lectures To My Students* (Fig, 2012), 138.

max. Stop reading for a moment, and count to five seconds in your head. That felt pretty long, didn't it?

These dramatic pauses convey confidence and authority. They allow the reader's mind to digest what you just said. But too much silence can cause their mind's to drift.

Filler Words: The Pause's Mortal Enemy

When I took my first public speaking class in college, I was excited. I wanted to be a preacher. Public speaking was going to be my thing. I thought, "This class will be cake! I get to work on my skills and get an easy A."

When the professor called on me to give my first talk, I stood confidently and killed it! The best presentation ever. The class was speechless. If I had a microphone, I would have dropped it right there.

But when I sat down, the professor said the worst thing anyone can say after a presentation, "Any feedback class?"

For the next ten minutes, I listened in horror as each of my classmates ripped into me for all my bad habits. I said "um" every sentence. I looked at my notes almost the entire speech. And I gripped the podium on both sides like a man on a life raft off the Titanic.

The worst part was that I was clueless. I thought they were all liars. They were just jealous of my undeniable awesomeness. But then I watched the video. They were right! I had bad habits and didn't know it.

My question for you is this: Do you have any bad habits? How do you know?

I drove my car the other day to pick up my daughter from school. It is a familiar route that I drive almost every day. While driving, I must have been lost in thought about work stuff, because when I pulled up to the school, I realized that I had no recollection of how I got there.

Have you ever had this happen to you? You were driving, but your brain wasn't processing what you were doing. Why? Because your brain was focused on thinking about something else and the route is a habit. You've probably driven down that road a hundred times. When we do something habitually, we can do it without thinking much of it.

This is what often happens when we are preaching. We are so focused on what we are saying that our brain doesn't focus on familiar bad habits.

Here's the point: We need help discovering these bad preaching habits.

There are two ways to do this: Ask someone you trust to sit in the audience and watch for bad habits, or record yourself and find them yourself.

Every Monday morning, the first thing I do when I sit down in the office is to watch a recording of one of the services I preached on Sunday. I look for things I did well that I should keep doing. I look for things I can improve. And I watch for any bad habits that I have or may have developed.

One of the absolute best ways to improve as a communicator is to watch yourself. If you are not watching yourself preach every week, you are missing a huge opportunity for growth.

When you watch yourself, you will notice all the little things that you don't notice while you are in the middle of thinking about what to say next. All your flaws will come flying out to you. Don't be discouraged, though. Admitting you have a problem is the first step to fixing it.

The most common bad habits are filler words. You could prepare the greatest sermon on the planet, but filler words make you sound like you have no idea what you are talking about. You lose credibility.

Compare the following example:

- **Filler words:** "Jesus is, um, like, the only way to Heaven. So, uh, run to him."

- **No filler words:** "Jesus is the only way to Heaven. Run to him."

See the difference? Filler words hurt your credibility. They rob a preacher's message of its power and conviction.

So maybe you, um, OK, say, like, a lot of, you know, filler words, and stuff. What should you do?

How to Eliminate Filler Words

Calvin Miller says, "Work to eliminate all affectations of manner and voice in delivery. Of all the axioms this one is the very hardest to eliminate for it requires dividing your brain into two parts, one of which is delivering your sermon and the other of which is monitoring the delivery."[28]

Since we don't often realize our bad habits in the moment, the only way we will be able to kill them is to force ourselves into awareness.

---

[28]   Calvin Miller, *Preaching: The Art of Narrative Exposition* (Grand Rapids: Baker, 2006), 193.

You have to do something that will help your brain flag these activities. Being conscious of them will help you eliminate them.

Get a video camera. For this purpose, any camera will do. It doesn't have to be fancy. Set up the camera and record yourself while preaching.

Now, watch yourself like a hawk with a piece of scratch paper and a pen. Write the filler words you hear, and make a mark on the paper every time you hear that word.

For example, if you say "uh" a lot, count your "uh's." If you said it thirty times, that's OK. Next week the goal is to get that number down. Maybe next time you get down to twenty. That's great. You've made some serious progress.

Recording your bad habits is a great way to kill them. Why? Because in the back of your mind, you will know that you are going to be counting your habits. Your brain will start to become very aware of whenever you say these words.

The key here is to force your brain to think about the bad habits. If you want to be a better preacher, you have to work hard to eliminate anything that gets in the way of clear communication.

You can do this. You can become habit free. Trust me; your listeners will thank you.

Follow the Action Step below to help kill filler words and replace them with the sweet silence of a pause.

ACTION STEP: Count Your Filler Words

Follow the process explained above. Record your next sermon. Then, like my professor did for me in class, look for all your filler words and keep count of them. Put a mark on the page every time you hear the filler word. Count your total.

Your goal next week is to lower your filler word total and replace them with pauses.

Record yourself again and count for yourself, or ask someone in audience to keep track for you while you preach and report to you with the total.

Get that number down. You can do it!

6. STRUCTURE: Start Fast; Finish Strong

There are three types of preachers: those to whom you cannot listen; those to whom you can listen; and those to whom you must listen. During the introduction the congregation usually decides the kind of speaker addressing them that morning.

— Haddon Robinson[29]

---

[29] Haddon W. Robinson, *Biblical Preaching: The Development and Delivery of Expository Messages* (Grand Rapids: Baker, 2001) 175.

Like all stories, every sermon has a beginning, a middle, and an end. We cannot overlook the importance of this basic structure.

The beginning needs to grab your attention. The middle needs to hold your interest. The end needs to resolve the story (or the message) in a memorable way.

We know this intuitively about stories. If a story starts slow, meanders in the middle, or has an odd ending, we are disappointed. Sermons are similar.

Too many sermons have dragging introductions, rambling middles, and lazy conclusions.

The Introduction

First impressions matter. Within seconds, your audience will make hundreds of tiny judgments about you and your message based on the introduction alone.

The biggest problems I see with most introductions is that they start slow, run long, and worse yet, they don't answer the two primary question people have at the beginning of your sermon: "What is the message about?" and "Why should I care?"

There are two elements to a good introduction:

1. Start fast

Try to keep your introduction under 2 or 3 minutes—only a few paragraphs in your manuscript. You should be able to say everything you need to in a few minutes. But it requires a ruthless editing process to cut everything that's not necessary.

I love how H.B. Charles Jr. says it in his book, *On Preaching*:

> *"You want your introduction to be clean and tight and strong. Don't undermine it by stuffing it with too much material. The body of the message should be filled with good meat. The introduction should be fat free. So make sure everything in the introduction has a real purpose for being there. Know why every sentence is there, and ruthlessly edit out whatever does not fit."*[30]

Introductions that take forever cause people's minds wander to lunch or Fantasy Football.

What are you talking about? Why should I care? How does this impact me? These are questions people in the audience want to know. You will lose people if

---

[30] H.B. Charles Jr., *On Preaching: Personal & Pastoral Insights for the Preparation & Practice of Preaching*, Kindle ed. (Chicago: Moody, 2014), Location 926.

you ramble for ten minutes before they have a clue what the topic of your sermon is.

Most of us have a tendency to ease into a sermon. We've all heard it before: "Well, good morning everyone. It is so good to see you all today. Wasn't the music just great today? Can we all just give a round of applause to our amazing worship team? Amen. We are so blessed. Well, as you just heard in the announcement earlier, we are collecting food for the big church food drive. We couldn't be more excited about that. I look forward to this time every single year, and this year we have a goal to donate more than ever. Well, anyway, today we continuing our series, Awesome Sauce. We are in the second week today, and didn't pastor David do an excellent job last week? Wow, what a great word! So, today, we are going to be talking about..."

I know announcements can be important. I know the band probably did a great job. But the introduction is the most crucial moment of a sermon. People in the audience are only going to give you a minute to decide whether they want to listen or think about all the other things they have to do.

Bryan Chapell says that "audiences generally decide within the first thirty seconds of a presentation whether they are interested in what a speaker will say."[31] If that's true, do you really want to spend those thirty seconds repeating the announcements?

Instead of sliding into your sermon, you need to start with a bang—like a bullet from a gun.

Think about the last time you went to a movie where it took forever to get to the story. You were bored out of your mind for the first fifteen minutes, thinking, "get to the good stuff already!" Some of the best movies start right in the middle of the action. You are immediately thrust into a car chase, a bank robbery, a struggle for life and death, a hilarious situation, a murder, or a mysterious new world.

Your introduction should be no different. Begin in the middle of the action.

Start with a compelling question, a quick story (that gets to the point), a shocking statistic, or by describing a scenario your audience has experienced before. Mix it up and be creative. But jump right into the topic.

The first words from your mouth should be powerful. They should compel your audience to want to hear more. For example:

---

[31] Bryan Chapell, *Christ-Centered Preaching: Redeeming the Expository Sermon*, Kindle ed. (Grand Rapids: Baker, 2015), Location 5278.

- "Have you ever felt like no matter how hard you fight to get ahead, your life seems like one step forward, and three steps back?"

- "We thought it was going to be the best day our lives. We were on our honeymoon, relaxing on the beach, but then it happened..."

- "A recent study found that 65% of students involved in church in high school will walk away from their faith in college. 65%!"

2. Identify a problem

I was reading a classic children's book to my daughter, Ashlyn, before bed the other night, and I noticed something good writers do. At the end of every chapter, the author created suspense. The chapter would end in the middle of the action, or with an unresolved question (a mystery).

"I have to know what happens next, Daddy," Ashlyn begged. "Please, read more." She had to know how it ended. This little trick of creating a problem that needed a resolution made the book a page turner.

Like all good stories, your sermon needs an unresolved problem to hold your audience's attention. As Tim Keller says, "In your sermons you must build some suspense that creates an eagerness to hear what is coming next and a sense of traveling to a destination."[32]

As I mentioned earlier, there are two questions that people have at the beginning of a sermon: What is the message about, and why should I care?

When you identify a problem, you get right to the point. You tell your audience that your message will provide the solution to this issue. As Andy Stanley explains, "Your introduction should raise the question you are going to answer, create the tension you are going to resolve, or point to the mystery you are going to solve."[33] This tension of an unresolved problem or unanswered question makes a compelling introduction.

Begin by stirring up a problem that people face based on the topic of sermon: They cannot get out of debt. Their marriage is on the rocks. They feel distant from God. They are doubting their faith. They want more out of life.

---

[32] Timothy Keller, *Preaching: Communicating Faith in an Age of Skepticism*, Kindle ed. (New York: Penguin, 2015), 202.

[33] Andy Stanley, *Communicating for a Change: Seven Keys to Irresistible Communication* (Colorado Springs: Multnomah, 2006), 154.

Then, show how big the problem really is. What could happen if it's not solved? What are the consequences of not fixing the problem? What might life be like if the problem were finally gone?

Highlighting the problem creates tension in the room. People will nod their heads in agreement. "Yes, that's a problem I'm dealing with." At that moment, you have answered their question about why they should care. The sermon is about something they need.

People are self-centered. They want a sermon that relates to them. It's human nature. Sure, they may be happy if it helps other people too, but when you get down to it, people care most about themselves. Tap into this self-centeredness in the introduction. As Spurgeon said, "Self-interest quickens attention. Preach upon practical themes, pressing, present, personal matters, and you will secure an earnest hearing."[34]

The point of the introduction is not to solve the problem. The point is to identify the problem, so people know what the sermon is about, and are eager to learn what the Bible says about it.

_____

34   Charles H. Spurgeon, *Lectures To My Students* (Fig, 2012), 138.

The Body

The body of the sermon is the bulk of the message. It's the meaty middle. The most common pitfall I see in the body is that pastors try to cram in too much. So the sermon rambles and runs too long.

It's a rare thing to find a preacher who can hold an audience captive for more than an hour. Yes, there are some who do it well, but do their people love it or tolerate it?

If I'm sitting in on a sermon that runs over thirty minutes, my attention starts to drift. And I'm a pastor who loves listening to preaching! If it's difficult for me, what about the average churchgoer?

Most people today struggle to listen to someone talk for longer than 30 minutes. To keep our attention, it had better be entertaining (like a great comedian), or incredibly impactful (think of the best sermon you have ever heard).

Most often, we preach long because we have so much we would like to say. We want to deliver every piece of information we have discovered in our study. But isn't it better to leave the audience wanting more than wishing for less?

If you are a long-winded preacher, I challenge you to test this. Survey random people in your church.

Ask for honest feedback on the length of your sermons. If you want accurate results, make the survey anonymous. The people who love you will be too kind to you otherwise.

I don't buy the idea that sermons for people have to be short to hold their attention. People can sit through a 30-45 minute message. But it has to be interesting, and it has to keep moving.

If you tell a story that takes too long to get to the point, you will lose people. Listening to a pastor ramble for 15-20 minutes without getting to the point is torturous.

A rambling pastor is usually a result of poor preparation. They have either prepared too much information or too little.

Too much information

Maybe you become a historian when you introduce a passage of Scripture. You describe the architecture, the types of clothing people wore, the political climate, and every last ounce of historical detail you can.

Yes, you did your homework. Yes, you are thorough. But most people don't care. Give people enough information to set up the passage. Then, let Scripture speak for itself. Only provide details essential to understanding the meaning of the text. You will have to explain some historical details, but don't get carried away.

If you take too long setting up a passage of scripture, you will lose people. It's a sermon, not a history class. Your goal should be to point people to the Bible, not prove how smart you are.

I recently sat in on a sermon where the pastor preached so many different points with so many different fill-in-the-blanks that I got lost. I seriously had no idea what exactly this man was talking about, because I missed the point in all the points.

If you have too much to say, split your sermon into two or three messages. Don't cram too much into one talk.

Keep the body of the sermon simple. What's the one big, overarching idea that people need to understand from this passage of scripture?

Stick to the point, or you will lose people in information overload.

Lack of preparation

Maybe you had an insane week. You were so busy that you didn't prepare your sermon like you wished you could have. So when you are on stage, you ramble.

You didn't plan your points well, so you say whatever comes to mind. And while you are trying to think about what to say next, you keep rambling to buy more time. As a result, you preach a longer sermon because you prepared less.

I love what Charles Spurgeon said: "If you ask me how you may shorten your sermons, I should say, study them better. Spend more time in the study that you may need less in the pulpit. We are generally longest when we have least to say."[35] It's so true.

Lack of preparation makes your preaching scatterbrained. Your audience is confused about where you are going because you don't even know.

This is why I'm a firm believer in the "5 P's" of preaching: Proper preparation prevents poor preaching.

After you write the message, you have to cut all details that aren't necessary. Eliminate anything that is too repetitive. Kill tangents. Trim your stories to only the essential information. Get to the point, and stay there.

You need to know exactly how long you have to preach and make sure that the body of the sermon

---

[35] Spurgeon, *Lectures*, 138.

doesn't leave you with no time for your conclusion. Because when it does, you will have to end too fast.

If you want to learn more about preparing a sermon, you may enjoy my book *Preaching Nuts & Bolts*.

The Conclusion

The biggest problem I see in sermon conclusions are that they end weak.

Do not make the mistake of overlooking the importance of your conclusion. You've spent the last 25-45 minutes preaching your guts out. The final moment of your sermon needs to be strong.

The conclusion is your final word on the matter. It should be the strongest point and most memorable part of the message. Don't waste it.

There are two common reasons that conclusions get weak: the preacher ran out of time and had to end abruptly, or they were lazy and didn't work to write a strong conclusion, so they keep talking in circles until finally coming to a halt.

1. Abrupt endings: The pastor is preaching, and the sermon clock is flashing red. The people in the sound booth keep pointing to their watch, saying, "Wrap it up!" Finally, the pastor looks at the clock and realizes that he's out of time. So he finishes his sentence, and says, "Well, looks like we are out of time today. Let's pray."

Although this approach may be better than a lazy conclusion, your abrupt ending failed to capitalize on one of the most important parts of the sermon. You missed the chance to drive the message home.

2. Lazy conclusions: Too often, when a pastor says, "In conclusion," it doesn't signal the end of the message. The audience knows better. He's not about to end. Instead, he's going to preach another 10-15 minutes and throw in a few bonus sermon points.

The pastor has a lazy conclusion. It's a similar problem to easing into the introduction. He doesn't know exactly how he wants to end the message. He didn't work hard to craft the conclusion. Like an old dog, he walks in circles until he finds a place to rest. He keeps repeating things he already said until he finally eases into a closing prayer.

End strong

The best conclusions are neither abrupt or lazy, but deliberate. They summarize the main point and drive it home (sometimes with an inspiring story).

Like a hammer to a nail, you need to hit the central point until you drive it into the mind of your audience. (We will discuss how to preach in a memorable way in Chapter 9).

Presentation expert Nancy Duarte says, "In order to get the most out of the audience, describe the possible future outcomes with wonder and awe. Show the audience that the reward will be worth their efforts."[36] Her advice applies to sermon conclusions too. Paint an inspiring picture of what the future may look like if people apply God's Word to their life.

Summarize your sermon, cast a vision for a desirable future, challenge the audience to take action, and end with a memorable closing statement.

Don't add more ideas. Just hammer your main point home. As Haddon Robinson says, "Don't introduce new material in the conclusion. These final moments should drive home what you have said, and they should not take the audience off into new avenues of thought. A sermon moves the guns into position. Now is the time to fire the shot at the listener's mind and emotions."[37]

---

[36] Nancy Duarte, *Resonate: Present Visual Stories that Transform Audiences*, Kindle ed. (Hoboken: Wiley, 2010), Location 1006.

[37] Robinson, *Biblical Preaching*, 180.

The closing statement may be a phrase you have repeated throughout the message, scripture, a quote, a story, a challenge, or whatever else fits.

Remember, the last thing you say in a sermon is often the most memorable. Work hard on crafting and memorizing a great closing statement, so you don't leave everyone with, "Well, umm, that's all I've got today. So, uh, let's pray."

ACTION STEP: Write Your Intro and Conclusion

Write the introduction and conclusion for your next sermon word-for-word using what you learned in this chapter.

Start with a bang. Jump right into the problem, and end strong. Also, don't forget to practice the introduction and conclusion before you preach.

Record your sermon and compare your introduction and conclusion to the previous week. Was there a difference? Was the sermon better? How else might you improve?

7. CLARITY: Speak Simply

Pray that I will proclaim this message as clearly as I should.

— The Apostle Paul[38]

In 1990 a Stanford University psychology experiment, led by Ph.D. student Elizabeth Newton, assigned groups of two people to play a simple game. One person would be the "tapper." The other would be the "listener."

The tapper was asked to choose a simple song that everyone would know like "Happy Birthday to You." Then, by only tapping the rhythm of the song

---

[38]   Colossians 4:4 NLT

on a table, their job was to help the listener guess the name of the song.

Before the game started, the tappers were asked to predict their success rate. They predicted that the listener would get 50% of the songs correct.

To their surprise, the listeners only guessed the song correct three times out of 120 attempts (a measly 2.5% success rate).[39]

What happened?

The tappers had what Chip and Dan Heath, in their book *Made to Stick*, call the Curse of Knowledge. While tapping the song, the tappers heard the melody in their heads. They knew the song, so the answer was obvious to them.

The listeners, on the other hand, did not have the same knowledge as the tappers. They only heard rhythmic tapping. A rhythm is far different than a melody.

Go ahead and try this game for yourself. It's almost impossible!

Chip and Dan explain: "This is the Curse of Knowledge. Once we know something, we find it hard to imagine what it was like not to know it. Our knowl-

---

[39]   Chip Heath and Dan Heath, *Made to Stick: Why Some Ideas Survive and Others Die*, Kindle ed. (New York: Random House, 2007), Location 300.

edge has 'cursed' us. And it becomes difficult for us to share our knowledge with others, because we can't readily re-create our listeners' state of mind."[40]

Here's the point: We all have the Curse of Knowledge.

Pastors know too much. Many of us have years of college level Bible study under our belts. A lot of us have even studied at a master's or even doctoral level.

We know all the stories. We've read the book many times. We are tough to beat in a game of Bible trivia.

If we are not careful, like the tappers, we will preach with the illusion that the audience understands us. In our mind, the point of our sermon is clear. We allude to Bible characters, speak in Christian terminology, and expect everyone in the audience to understand like we do.

But your listeners do not have the same knowledge you do. Biblical literacy in America is at an all-time low.

And what if you are trying to reach people who don't know Jesus? They have likely never read the entire Bible, much less a few chapters. They got a degree

---

[40]   Heath, *Made to Stick*, Location 318.

in business, architecture, graphic design, or how to party.

This is why many pastors preach, but few connect. The Curse of Knowledge sneaks into our sermons. We take our years of study for granted, and it clouds our message.

By the way, the Curse of Knowledge is not a new phenomenon. It's similar to what Martin Luther, one of the primary figures of the Protestant Reformation, was warning about when he said:

> "Cursed be every preacher who aims at lofty topics in the church, looking for his glory and selfishly desiring to please one individual or another. When I preach here, I adapt myself to the circumstances of the common people. I don't look at the doctors and masters, of whom scarcely forty are present, but I look at the hundred or the thousand young people and children. It's to them that I devote myself, for they, too, need to understand. If the others don't want to listen they can leave. Therefore... take pains to be simple and direct; don't consider those who claim to be learned but be a preacher to the unschooled youth and sucklings."[41]

[41] John T. Pless, "Martin Luther: Preacher of the Cross," Concordia Theological Quarterly 51 (1987): 91-92.

To communicate well, our words need to be clear and simple. But preaching simply is not so simple. As Luther said, "To preach simply is a great art."[42] It requires hard work and dedication.

Breaking the Curse

Breaking the Curse of Knowledge begins with awareness. If anything in your message assumes that the listener has any prior knowledge, you will struggle to connect. You are tapping "Happy Birthday to You."

Simple preaching doesn't mean you have to water down the message. It means you have to teach as if those listening to your message know nothing about God, Christianity, or the Bible.

You can take the message deep, but you need to start with the people in the kiddie pool and ease them into the deep end.

So think about the non-believer in the back row. This may be your one and only shot to reach that person.

You must know who you are speaking to, and what they don't know. Then, you can think about the

---

[42]   Arthur Skevington Wood, *Captive to the Word: Martin Luther, Doctor of Sacred Scripture* (Exeter: Paternoster Press, 1969), 92.

words and phrases that you know and take for granted that need to be explained.

Theological Words Need Explanation

As a general rule, any time you use a theological word, you should define it. If you are saying a lot of words like "sanctification," "transubstantiation," "regeneration," "incarnation," or any other ten-dollar word you learned in seminary, you are losing people if you don't explain the meaning. If there's an "ation" in the word, that should be your first hint that you better define it or use another word.

Don't make people feel like they need a dictionary or a seminary degree to understand what you are talking about.

Even words that you might think are common knowledge like "gospel," "sin," "glory," and "salvation" need explanation for a newcomer. What you picture in your mind when saying "sin" could be very different that what other people picture.

Go ahead and use technical terms if you want, but define them in simple terms. This doesn't mean you have to say, "Webster's dictionary defines 'sin' as..." A small interjection may be enough: "Our sin, any failure to follow God's moral law, will lead to destruction."[43]

This may get a little tiresome for you because you already know what you are talking about. But that's the Curse of Knowledge. You cannot assume that everyone in the audience is on the same page because most of them probably aren't.

Repeating these definitions week after week will only help your audience grow in their understanding of theology.

Speaking Christianese

My wife, Taryn, is a nurse. Anyone who knows a medical professional knows that they speak in a different language around each other. Whenever I go out to dinner with my wife and her nurse or doctor friends, I'm lost. For example, most people would say, "puke," but they say, "emesis." And that's about all I know. So I just nod my head and smile. If there is another spouse there who isn't in the medical field, we just look at each other and laugh. We're both clueless.

All groups develop a shared language in time. Christianity is no different. You may not know this,

---

43   See "sin" as defined in Wayne Grudem, *Systematic Theology: An Introduction to Biblical Doctrine*, Kindle ed. (Grand Rapids: Zondervan, 1994), Location 32659.

but you are fluent in Christianese. Christianese is the insider language that church people fluently speak that may sound confusing or odd to non-Christians.

Have you ever thought about how many people feel like outsiders in Christian circles because they do not know the lingo? Walking through the doors of a church is intimidated enough for most people. They already feel like an outsider. They are already questioning whether or not your church is a place where they fit in.

Speaking Christianese from the stage is a quick way to confirm, "Yes, you are an outsider. And no, you don't fit in here."

Christian terminology is not a new problem in the church. In fact, did you know that Christians were falsely accused of cannibalism in the early church because Romans (the outsiders) heard they were drinking the blood and eating the body of Christ in their gatherings? Now that is a serious misunderstanding!

Christians in the early days were also accused of incest because they called one another "brother" and "sister." So when a "brother" married a "sister," people were concerned.

Look, we have the most important message in the world. Life and death are literally in the balance. We must be clear with the words we use and how we communicate to newcomers.

I'm not saying that we shouldn't use these phrases. Some of them are straight from the Bible. But when we use them, we had better provide a simple definition.

There are countless examples I could give of Christianese language that we say all the time. Here are just twelve of them to consider:

1. **"Fellowship"** Only Christians call hanging out together fellowshipping. Those outside the church may think you are referring to a work program for on-the-job training.

2. **"Quiet Time"** Is that like putting your kid in time out? Christians may know that you mean time spent in prayer and reading God's word (usually in the morning with a cup of coffee), but non-Christians don't.

3. **"Hedge of Protection"** How much protection does a hedge even provide? I for one would rather have some bulletproof glass protection or maybe castle with a moat protection.

4. **"Small Group" / "Home Group" / "Life Group" / "Missional Community Group"** ... It seems every church has a different name for their groups. Whatever you brand them, explain what they are. These names mean nothing to outsiders.

5. **"Traveling Mercies"** What is a traveling mercy anyway? Nobody outside of the church talks like this. Could you just say "safe trip" instead?

6. **"Washed by the Blood" / "Saved by the Blood of the Lamb"** Could anything sound more like a cult to an outsider than the mental image of people getting washed in sheep blood? Gross.

7. **"Anointed"** Where would a person ever hear this word outside of Christian circles? Usually, you are trying to say that a person has a God-given ability.

8. **"Hallelujah"** Most people today know that Hallelujah is a word Christians say when they

are praising God for something. But still, I doubt the average guest at your church is fluent in Hebrew.

9. **"Tithe" / "Tithing" / "Tithes and Offerings"** It is intimidating enough to a newcomer that you are asking them to give you money. The least you could do is clarify the words you use when you do it.

10. **"Communion" / "Lord's Supper" / "Lord's Table" / "Eucharist"...** We have a lot of words for the Christian ritual of eating stale crackers with a shot of grape juice. Don't assume that everyone knows what you mean, even Christians from a different church tradition.

11. **"Lay Hands On"** Does this sound a bit violent to anyone else? It sounds similar to the phrase "don't lay a hand on me." Of course, Christians know you mean prayer, but they are the insiders.

12. **"Body of Christ"** Are you talking about Jesus' physical body, the stale crackers we serve with grape juice, or a metaphor for the church?

This list is not comprehensive. There are many other Christianese words and phrases we use without thinking twice about them.

Tim Keller adds that "you should not use unexplained theological terms like 'hermeneutics,' 'eschatological,' 'covenant,' 'kingdom,' or even 'theological' repeatedly. If you do, not only will outsiders to the faith be confused, but Christians will intuitively know not to bring their less initiated friends to hear you."[44]

Think about the words and phrases we could add to this list. What terminology do you speak that you need to watch out for?

Our goal should be to preach as Paul said: "we do not use deception, nor do we distort the word of God. On the contrary, by setting forth the truth *plainly* we commend ourselves to everyone's conscience in the sight of God" (2 Corinthians 4:2 NIV, emphasis added).

---

44   Timothy Keller, *Preaching: Communicating Faith in an Age of Skepticism*, Kindle ed. (New York: Penguin, 2015), 77.

Speak simply. Use the common language of your audience, so the good news will be clear for all to hear.

ACTION STEP: Make a Dictionary

Open a word document and create a list of definitions for common Christianese words and theological terms that you use. Simplify these definitions as much as possible so that your people will be able to understand them.

Consult a resource like a theological dictionary to help. I recommend looking at the glossary of terms in the back of Wayne Grudem's *Systematic Theology*. Unlike many theology books, Grudem's definitions are purposefully written in a simple and clear manner for all to understand.

Now, for you next sermon, open this document. Copy and paste your definitions where needed.

8. ENGAGEMENT: Invite Involvement

Despite the fondest wishes of a preacher, most parishioners struggle to pay attention to each word from the pulpit, just as most preachers do when they happen to sit in the pew.

— *Bryan Chapell*[45]

I started in ministry as a worship leader. If you've ever led people in worship, you know that an engaged crowd is so much better than a disengaged one. The worship experience feels more powerful when people clap, sing along, or raise their hands. It's awkward when nobody sings with you.

---

[45] Bryan Chapell, *Christ-Centered Preaching: Redeeming the Expository Sermon*, Kindle ed. (Grand Rapids: Baker, 2015), Location 7678.

I will never forget the times when I led worship as a student in my high school youth ministry. I played the guitar and sang every Wednesday and Sunday. But there were many times when nobody engaged in the experience. Sometimes students would just stand and stare at me. Sometimes they would be talking to the person next to them. And on more than one occasion, an impromptu game of dodgeball erupted in the middle of the song as a rowdy student began throwing balls at people and running around the room.

No matter what I did, there was not the culture of engagement in worship that I longed for. It broke my heart, but I kept singing and strumming my guitar trying to give glory to God. And to be fair, I was not a very engaging worship leader in these early days either. I often stared at my notes because I didn't know the songs.

Years later, I became the youth pastor of a church, and it was like worship deja vu. The students in my ministry stared lifelessly into the distance during worship. It had to change.

As their new leader, it was my responsibility to do something about it. I got more involved leading worship. I coached the student worship team on how to be more engaging. I took away their notes, so they had to learn the song and look at the audience instead of a sheet of paper. I also recruited adult leaders and asked them to model the kind of worship engagement we wanted our students to have.

Finally, while leading worship, I began to coach the students how to engage. I said things like:

- "Sing this part with me."

- "Clap with me."

- "Everyone raise your hands with me and sing at the top of your lungs."

And the culture slowly changed. Over the course of a year, the students began to engage in worship. Before long, a small group of apathetic students routinely engaged in authentic worship.

No, they didn't all clap. They didn't all raise their hands. They didn't all sing. But we created a culture where students were invited to engage in the music and unashamedly sing praise to their creator.

Think about the difference between these two scenarios. In the first instance, I expected engagement but did nothing to encourage it. In the second instance, I modeled and encouraged engagement.

The same lesson I learned about worship engagement applies to your preaching as well.

Is Your Audience Engaged?

Do people respond to your preaching? Do they laugh at jokes? Do they say "Amen?" Do they ever clap their hands? Are they leaning in? Are they taking notes? Do they read their Bibles along with you?

You may think the problem is your church tradition. Maybe you come from a church tradition that doesn't expect audience interaction. Nobody even raises their hands or claps during worship. Shoot, people barely even sing.

You may think the problem is your people. They just are not on fire for the Lord. They don't get it. They are hard-hearted and stubborn folk. They are more intellectual than emotional.

While either of these cases may be true, I want to propose something different. If your audience is dull, maybe the problem isn't your audience or your church tradition. Maybe the problem is you. Maybe you haven't engaged them.

Audience engagement starts with the preacher. Most people will do what you ask, but many pastors never ask. The church traditions that are highly engaged have a history of pastors who encouraged engagement.

We have to understand that good preaching rests somewhere between monolog and dialogue (a lecture and a conversation). The preacher does the talking, but the audience gives feedback with their body language, and sometimes their mouths.

Now, to be clear, I need to make a few important disclaimers:

1. Just because people say, "Amen!" or applaud you, doesn't mean you're a better preacher.

2. Audience engagement will look different by church tradition. An engaged Presbyterian will probably respond differently than an engaged Pentecostal, and that's OK. Engagement for your tradition may be a person shouting, "Hallelujah!" or it may be a subtle nodding of the head in agreement.

3. There is no better way to engage an audience than a great message. A bad sermon negates all the tips in this chapter. If your preaching is

bad, boring, or unbiblical, engagement isn't the problem.

So how do you help build audience engagement? I have found five ways that are helpful.

1. Ask questions

When you only speak at people, they will either tune you out or listen passively. By asking questions, you engage people's minds. You invite them to think for themselves instead of letting you do all the thinking for them.

Have you ever noticed that Jesus asked a lot of questions? Rather than telling everyone the answer, Jesus led his listeners to the answer by asking a lot of questions. For examples, see Matthew 16:26, or 22:20-21.

Questions are a powerful teaching method, especially when teaching to hostile or skeptical people. Questions stimulate critical thinking, and good questions make the audience long for answers. They invite people to participate in the sermon because they ask people to think with you. So in your sermon, don't just tell people the answers; Lead them to discover the truth by asking the right questions.

Most of the time your questions will be rhetorical—you aren't expecting people to answer aloud. But there may be times when you want your audience to give an audible response. In these cases, make it clear that you want an answer. You may want to motion your hands toward yourself or cup your hand behind your ear.

Like Jesus, great preachers ask great questions. Don't underestimate the power of a well-timed question in your sermon.

2. Tell them how to respond

If you want people to respond a certain way to your sermon, ask them to. It may feel strange at first, but your audience will do what you ask them to do if it's not too far out of their comfort zone.

Here are a few examples:

- "Raise your hands if..."

- "Amen?"

- "Nod your head if you agree that..."

- "Tell the person next to you..."

- "Look at this..."

- "Let's give a round of applause for..."

- "Listen close, because this is important..."

- "Stand up if..."

- "Repeat after me..."

- "Close your eyes and imagine this with me...."

- "Every head bowed..."

You can also invite people to respond without saying anything. If you do certain things, people will know that you are asking them to do it with you.

For example, if you ask a question like, "How many of us have ever felt like that?" and raise your hand, people in the audience will raise their hands too. Or if you say a powerful, true statement and then nod your head, people in the audience will nod along with you. Not everyone will follow, but these subtle visual cues let your audience know that you want them to respond.

Most people in the audience are self-conscious. They don't want to do or say anything that will draw attention. They need to know that engagement is OK and encouraged. So unless you invite them to participate, and others join in, they will default to no inter-action.

Here's the bottom line: People will often do what you ask them to do. Don't assume that they will respond the way you expect. Be clear about what you want them to do, and they will do it.

3. Use visual illustrations

We could all learn a valuable lesson from kinder-garten; you have to show and tell. Many pastors tell but don't show.

Give people something to look at. We are visual beings. Visuals catch our eyes and engage our brains.

Look at Jesus. He often used object lessons to communicate concrete truth to his listeners.

- He washed the feet of the disciples to teach servant leadership (John 13:3–17).

- He called a little child to him to discuss child-like faith (Matthew 18:1–4).

- He described unselfish giving after watching a widow drop two small coins into the temple offering (Mark 12:41–44).

- Even when he told the parable of the sower, there's a good chance he was standing near a field.

Follow Jesus' example. Turn analogies and metaphors into visual illustrations. If you have a major point you are trying to make, ask yourself, "How can I demonstrate this?" It may not work in every message, but I guarantee people will be more engaged when it does.

Visually communicated truth is far stronger than just verbally spoken truth. So try using objects, pictures, and videos. Take time to be creative and think of ways to communicate your message visually, not just verbally.

4. Add humor

Humor immediately draws people in. It also disarms a tough crowd.

Laughter is a natural reaction of an audience engaged in a story or joke. You cannot laugh at something and not be engaged. It's impossible.

Laughter is also contagious. Have you ever noticed that watching a funny movie is always better with a crowd? We feed off the laughter of others.

Warning: This doesn't mean to tell a bunch of corny preacher jokes that you find on the internet. I'm talking about using your natural sense of humor when appropriate. *(We will discuss humor more in chapter 11.)*

5. Tell stories

People love stories. We live in one of the most story-centered cultures of all time. Movies, TV, books, talk shows, sports, music, magazines... all of them tell stories.

People naturally engage with stories, because we want to know what happens next. Plus, good stories engage an audience emotionally. A great story can bring people to laughter, tears, or cheers.

If your audience is drifting, tell a story, and they will snap back to attention. I often find that people remember my stories long after they've forgotten my sermons.

Plus, Jesus told a story or two himself. So there may be something to this.

Jesus told countless parables. He pulled spiritual truths from everyday life. Not only did these stories make his teaching more memorable, but they also connected in a much more profound way.

Think about the parable of the Prodigal Son. Jesus could have taught, "God loves you so much that He will welcome you back no matter how sinful you have lived."

Instead, Jesus tells the story of a boy who disowned his family, partied away his inheritance, came home to beg for mercy, but is surprisingly welcomed with open arms by his father who waited daily for his return.

The story is far more compelling. It tugs your heart and stirs your soul more than a mere statement.

So tell stories—lots of them. Use everyday life to teach profound spiritual truths like Jesus did.

Invite Involvement

Unless it's already part of your church's culture, your audience will be no more engaged in your sermon than you invite them to be.

If you want people to be more engaged, remember: it starts with preaching great sermons. But after that, you have to give people permission to interact with your message and encourage them to do it.

People love being part of the sermon, so find ways to include them. It's always better to have some level of involvement from the audience than telling them to sit still, shut up, and listen.

ACTION STEP: Add Interactive Elements

Include a few elements in your next sermon that invite audience engagement. Here are a few ideas:

- Take a poll by raising hands.

- Ask them to shout answers to a question.

- Invite a few people up on the stage to demonstrate a point.

- Ask the audience to do something: stand, sit, jump, close their eyes, look at something, make a noise, elbow their neighbor, play a game, dance, or sing.

Whatever you do, get creative and have fun. Then, record your sermon and evaluate the interactive elements.

Did it make the sermon better? Was the sermon more appealing? Did it help maintain or regain the audience's attention?

9. MEMORABILITY: Make Your Sermons Stick

Nobody remembers a paragraph. People are impacted by statements that stick... Take the time to reduce your one point to one sticky statement. It doesn't need to be cute. It doesn't have to rhyme. But it should be short and memorable. Your statement is your anchor... This will be what people remember.

— Andy Stanley[46]

---

[46] Andy Stanley, *Communicating for a Change: Seven Keys to Irresistible Communication* (Colorado Springs: Multnomah, 2006), 111.

When my daughter, Ashlyn, was four-years-old, one of her favorite TV shows was *Daniel Tiger's Neighborhood* on PBS. It's a modern spin-off of the classic *Mister Rogers' Neighborhood*.

Like most kids shows, every episode teaches a lesson. But Daniel Tiger is different. Where most shows teach a lesson at the very end, Daniel Tiger sings the lesson in a short jingle in various moments throughout the show.

When Ashlyn first started watching, I didn't think much of it. But then something amazing happened. She began singing these jingles in different situations to help her make good choices.

Her little brother, Jaxon, would do something to make her mad. But before she blew up at him, she would sing, "When you get so mad that you want to ROAR... take a deep breath and count to four. 1, 2, 3, 4."

While we were busy doing something, she would suddenly stop say, "Daddy, I need to go potty." Then she would sing, "When you have to go potty, STOP, and go right away. Flush, and wash, and be on your way."

My favorite is when we would tell Ashlyn that she doesn't have a choice for dinner. She has to eat whatever we are eating. Instead of getting upset she would sing, "You gotta try new food, 'cause it might taste good."

These phrases have now become part of my family's vocabulary. For example, my wife and I often find ourselves reminding Ashlyn and Jaxon things like, "You get what you get, and you don't throw a fit."

Daniel Tiger became one of my favorite shows, not only because it helped my daughter, but because it has mastered the art of the memorable phrase.

The fact that these statements have stuck with Ashlyn, and helped to change her behavior is nothing short of amazing. Every pastor should watch this show and take notes. Not so we know when to go potty, but so we can learn how to use memorable phrases in our preaching.

What would happen if we preached more like this? I'm not suggesting that you break out into song in every sermon or start writing jingles, but what if we all were as good as Daniel Tiger at crafting and repeating memorable phrases?

- When people in our church were about to face a tough situation, what if a phrase from a sermon popped into their heads?

- What if every youth pastor was able to craft these kinds of statements into their sermons so teenagers could recall Biblical wisdom in the face of peer pressure?

- What if our children's ministries used memorable statements like these to teach our children Biblical principles?

This practice is nothing new. For centuries, Christians have written hymns and creeds to help people remember Biblical teachings and theological principles. Why? Because memorable phrases stick with you and pop up when you need them.

The Six Principles of a Memorable Message

All preachers want their message to stick. We want our audience to remember the sermon. Who wants to spend hours every week to prepare a message that nobody remembers?

So, what makes a sermon sticky? What makes a memorable message?

Years ago, I read a great book by Chip, and Dan Heath called *Made to Stick* that answers this question.

They share their findings after studying thousands of messages that have stood the test of time.

They discovered six principles that make a message sticky. The stickiest messages are simple, unexpected, concrete, credible, emotional, stories (forming the acronym "SUCCESs").[47] Not every sticky message has to contain every principle, but the more it has, the stickier it will be.

Think about each of these principles of a memorable message.

1. **Simple:** The message was not too long and got to the core idea. Think of the difference between a nursery rhyme and the lecture of a college professor. The simple message is easier to recall.

2. **Unexpected:** The message was surprising. It took an unexpected twist or arrived at a shocking conclusion. When surprised, we naturally retain more information as our eyes widen and we snap to attention.

---

[47] Chip Heath and Dan Heath, *Made to Stick: Why Some Ideas Survive and Others Die*, Kindle ed. (New York: Random House, 2007), Location 288.

3. **Concrete:** The message contained concrete words, not abstract ideas. For example, think about which of the following is easier to remember: "It's better for you to be content with what you already have than to risk losing what you already have while trying to get something bigger." Or, "A bird in the hand is worth two in the bush."

4. **Credible:** The message came from either a credible source, facts, convincing details, or just sounded trustworthy. If people don't believe the source of a message or at least agree that it sounds true, they won't care to remember it.

5. **Emotional:** The message made people feel something. The emotions could range to anything from anger, happiness, sadness, disgust, or resentment. We remember things that trigger our emotions.

6. **Stories:** The message told a story. Stories are easy to remember, more interesting and can

provide examples of how we should change our behavior or react in different situations. Calvin Miller says that "all listeners hear with words but store what we hear in pictures. So sermons are remembered only if they contain enough pictures to be stored."[48]

What I find most interesting about these principles of sticky messages is that Jesus knew it long before Chip and Dan Heath did.

Jesus, Master of Memorable Phrases

Think about it. Jesus was a master of sticky ideas.

He often spoke poetically, using catchy sayings and plays on words. It's not always apparent in English translations. However, in the original language, Jesus made it much easier for his listeners to remember what he said.

And remember, Jesus never wrote any of his messages down. They were so memorable that his followers were able to recall them later. And here we are,

---

[48] Calvin Miller, *Preaching: The Art of Narrative Exposition* (Grand Rapids: Baker, 2006), 145.

over 2,000 years later, and you can quote many of them with minimal effort.

With Jesus' words translated from Greek into hundreds of other languages around the world, the message still sticks.

His teaching is full of simple, unexpected, concrete, credible, emotional, stories. I believe Jesus did it on purpose.

Jesus knowingly taught in a memorable way so that his message would continue to stick with us over 2,000 years later in every language around the world. Let that thought sink in for a moment.

Let's look at some examples:

Jesus' messages were simple

"Love your neighbor as yourself" (Matthew 19:19).

Jesus spoke in simple ways to simple people. For the most part, it doesn't take a college degree to understand Jesus' teaching. Most of his concepts can be summarized in a single sentence.

Jesus' messages were unexpected

"Blessed are the poor" (Matthew 5:3).

Jesus often used outrageous examples, exaggerations, or shocking statements to get people's attention. These statements were not all meant to be taken literally, but they got the point across.

For example, Jesus didn't mean that we literally have to rip out our eyes and amputate our hands for causing us to sin (Matthew 5:29-30). Otherwise, all Christians would be blind amputees.

He also didn't mean that the people he was speaking to had literal logs in their eyes (Matthew 7:3-5). He was making a point.

Jesus said unexpected things that shocked people to help us remember his point.

Jesus' messages were concrete

"If you have faith like a grain of mustard seed, you will say to this mountain, 'Move from here to there,' and it will move" (Matthew 17:20).

Jesus used concrete imagery—things you can see and touch—to explain abstract ideas. In the example above, he uses a mustard seed and a mountain to explain the abstract concept of faith.

Matthew 19:24 is another example: "It is easier for a camel to go through the eye of a needle than for a rich person to enter the kingdom of God." We can all imagine a camel trying to squeeze through the eye of a needle.

Jesus' messages were credible

"The crowds were astonished at his teaching, for he was teaching them as one who had authority" (Matthew 7:28-29).

Jesus' many miracles proved his authority. When a guy heals blind people, lepers, and even brings dead people back to life—much more raises himself from the dead—people are going to listen to what he has to say!

Plus, every word Jesus spoke were the very words of God. It doesn't get more credible than that.

Jesus' messages were emotional

"'Bring quickly the best robe, and put it on him, and put a ring on his hand, and shoes on his feet. And bring the fattened calf and kill it, and let us eat and celebrate. For this my son was dead, and is alive again; he was lost, and is found" (Luke 15:22-24).

Jesus knew how to engage people's emotions. Just think about the emotions in the parable of the Prodigal Son. The son walks home in shame, but the father runs to embrace him. And the older brother is furious. I've seen this story reduce grown men to tears. It's powerful.

Jesus' messages were stories

"He told them many things in parables" (Matthew 13:3).

Jesus was a master storyteller. Think about all of his parables: The prodigal son, the good Samaritan, the lost sheep, the sower and the seeds, and more.

Jesus knew how to weave a story to communicate his message in a memorable and powerful way. *(For more on this, see the next chapter.)*

Here's what we should learn from Jesus: Every preacher will benefit by making their sermons simple, unexpected, concrete, credible, and emotional by telling great stories.

The principles in *Made to Stick* are only pointing out what Jesus already knew and modeled for us.

If you want to preach in a memorable way, preach like Jesus.

How to Repeat One Big Idea Without Forcing It

My book, *Preaching Nuts & Bolts*, brought a ton of great questions from readers.

One reader, named Troy, asked the following: "I really enjoyed your book (just finished it). I left a review for you on Amazon. One quick question: I struggle with how to implement the one idea in my sermon over and over again in the same sermon without it coming across awkward. Any thoughts?"

What a great question! You may be thinking the same thing.

In the book, I suggested that every message should be focused on a single Big Idea drawn from the key Scripture of your sermon. You should be able to summarize your sermon in a sentence. That's the Big Idea. The more memorable, the better.

The question is, once you have the Big Idea, how do you inject it into your sermon without sounding forced or like a broken record?

I preached a sermon on parenting recently from Deuteronomy 6:4-9. The passage is about passing faith from one generation to the next.

After working through the process I explain in the book, I landed on the following Big Idea: *If you want your kids to follow Jesus every day of their lives, make him part of your everyday life.*

I began the sermon talking about how the number one goal of a Christian parent should be the spiritual well-being of their children. This was a perfect part to inject the first half of my Big Idea.

So I said something like this, "What should you do if you want your kids to follow Jesus every day of their lives? That is the big question. How can I help my kids follow Jesus every day of their lives?"

In the introduction, I had already repeated part of the Big Idea twice.

Then, we moved to the body of the sermon, diving into Deuteronomy 6:4-9 to find the answer.

After breaking down each verse, I paused and emphasized the Big Idea: *"If you want your kids to follow Jesus every day of their lives, make him part of your everyday life."*

Since I thought this was such a powerful phrase, I said, "Listen, you have to understand this. *If you want your kids to follow Jesus every day of their lives, make him part of your everyday life."*

After this, I moved into the application part of my message. I suggested four different times of day (from the text) that parents can use as an opportunity to teach their kids about Jesus. For each of these four times, I made my point and then repeated the Big Idea.

Finally, in the conclusion, I made sure to repeat it one last time as my closing words to end the message.

I find the best times to repeat the Big Idea are after you draw it out of Scripture, throughout the application, and again in the conclusion.

Make sure it's not forced. But don't waste an opportunity to repeat it anywhere it fits. The more you repeat it, the more they will remember it.

You may try asking your audience to repeat it after you. It can create some fun audience engagement, and help them remember it too.

You could also try deductive preaching—stating the big idea immediately and reinforcing it the rest of the sermon. But I gravitate towards inductive preaching—asking a question and taking my audience on a journey to discover the answer in Scripture.

My example above may sound a bit excessive. I don't always repeat the Big Idea that much. But when you have a powerful and memorable statement, the more you repeat it, the more likely people will be to remember it and, more importantly, apply it.

In fact, about a month after preaching this message, I had a conversation with someone who still remembered the phrase. I call that a win!

That's the power of preaching one memorable phrase. Do everything you can to help people remember your message.

ACTION STEP: Write a Memorable Phrase

Follow Jesus' example and craft a memorable phrase (Big Idea) for your next message based on the central passage of Scripture you are preaching. Run it through the SUCCESs acronym.

Is it simple? Is it unexpected? Is it concrete? Is it credible? Is it emotional? Is it part of a story?

You don't have to include every element. Don't force it. But the more you can include, the more memorable it will be.

Now, take that phrase and use it as the anchor for your sermon. Weave it in as much as you can.

Now preach it. Record it. And evaluate how memorable it was.

10. ILLUSTRATION: Show, Don't Tell

An illustration, like the picture on television, makes clear what the speaker explains.

— Haddon Robinson[49]

One Sunday morning, a pastor at a church I visited explained the Bible with the knowledge of a scholar. He highlighted words and details that I had never noticed before. As he finished the last verse of Scripture, my hand cramped from all the notes I scribbled. But then it ended. And something was missing.

"So what?" I thought. "I received some great knowledge today, but what do I do with all this? How

---

[49]   Haddon W. Robinson, *Biblical Preaching: The Development and Delivery of Expository Messages* (Grand Rapids: Baker, 2001) 152.

should this impact my life? How should this change me? How does this help me, encourage me, or guide me through another week living in a broken world?" I had to figure it out on my own.

Unfortunately, this is far too common in some churches today. Many pastors approach the church like an educational institution. After all, our job is to teach the Bible, right?

But if we are not careful, we teach Biblical information without Biblical application. Information without application doesn't inspire transformation.

Though people come to church wanting life transformation, they want it to be easy. Many want to know enough to save them without doing much to change them.

It's your job to do more than just teach the Bible. You must teach *and* apply.

Many sermons could be better if the preacher only spent a little more time on the application.

Like I did, you have to ask, "So what?"

So What?

Maybe you preach a lot of deep thoughts, abstract concepts, and sound doctrine. That's great. But even the best doctrinal teaching without real-life application will bore the snot out of most church-goers.

The whole time you are painting a theological masterpiece, they are asking, "So what? How does that affect me?"

Selfish? Yes. But true nonetheless.

The Bible is clear that application ought to be the result of hearing God's word. Paul writes, "For it is not the hearers of the law who are righteous before God, but the doers of the law who will be justified" (Romans 2:13 ESV) And James warns, "be doers of the word, and not hearers only, deceiving yourselves" (James 1:22 ESV). We do a great disservice to our audience when we fail to illustrate and apply the message in a way that inspires them to act on what they hear.

Go ahead and keep the abstract thoughts, but don't stop there. Answer the questions people are asking.

Continue to teach sound doctrine. Then say, "So what? How does this impact you and me?" and launch into some concrete, practical, real-world application, or an inspiring illustration. Not only will your people appreciate the practical tips and inspiration; they will begin to appreciate theology more as they see how it applies to everyday life.

Most preaching books separate illustration and application into different categories. But I believe they ought to be more linked than that.

John Stott reminds us that "The word 'illustrate' means to illuminate, to throw light on a dark object, and this is what our sermon illustrations should do. People find it very difficult to handle abstract ideas; we need to convert them either into symbols (as in mathematics) or into pictures."[50] Illustrations illuminate your sermon.

Illustrations are more than stories. They are more than entertainment. The purpose of an illustration is to help the listener see the point of the message with clarity so that they can apply it to their life. An illustration without an application is a contradiction.

Show. Don't tell.

Earlier this year, a major Christian website asked me to write an article for them. This organization is serious about their publishing, so they assigned me an editor.

---

[50] John Stott, *The Challenge of Preaching*, Kindle ed. (Cambridge: Wm. B. Eerdmans, 2013), Location 1102.

I felt conflicted. I was happy because I knew this would help me write a better article. But I was also nervous because nobody likes having their work critiqued. What if he doesn't like it? What if he thinks I'm a bad writer?

So I wrote the article, and awaited his response. Aside from some grammatical corrections, the editor had a major piece of advice scribbled throughout the article: "Show, don't tell."

I was telling people about things, but I wasn't showing it to them. For example, instead of writing, "The pastor was energetic." I should have described the pastor bounding across the stage, waving his arms over his head.

The editor, using standard advice for writers, helped me write better. And this made me think, how often do we do this in our preaching?

We tell people things, but we don't show them. Isn't that the key to great sermon application?

Jonathan Edwards, the great revivalist preacher of the First Great Awakening, argued that "human beings are body-bound creatures, and because of our fallenness, spiritual realities are simply not as real to us as sense experiences—things we actually see, hear, touch, smell, and taste."[51] We see this in his famous sermon, *Sinners in the Hands of an Angry God*. Edwards describes our righteousness having no more power to hold us from falling into hell than "a spider's web would have to stop a falling rock."[52] The spiritual truth becomes visible to us. We can see the rock crashing through the spider web because we've seen it before.

We need to do more than tell people what to do; we need to show them.

Example of Showing the Application

Let's say you are preaching on James 1:19-20, "Everyone should be quick to listen, slow to speak and slow to become angry, because human anger does not produce the righteousness that God desires" (ESV). Your Big Idea is straight from the text: anger doesn't produce righteousness.

---

[51] Timothy Keller, *Preaching: Communicating Faith in an Age of Skepticism*, Kindle ed. (New York: Penguin, 2015), 143.

[52] Jonathan Edwards, "Sinners in the Hands of an Angry God." Cited 15 January 2017. Online: http://edwards.yale.edu/archive?path=aHR0cDovL2Vkd2FyZHMueWFsZS5lZHUvY2dpLWJpbi9uZXdwaGlsby9nZXRRvbplY3QucGw/Yy4yMTo0Ny53amVv

Imagine yourself in the shoes of a particular group of people from a segment of your audience (such as parents, business people, single mothers, or twenty-somethings). Think about how this truth should impact their daily life. And think about more than just major life decisions. Reflect on the mundane tasks of everyday life too.

Putting yourselves in the shoes of your audience is not a new strategy. William Perkins, a sixteenth-century theologian at Cambridge "taught preachers to imagine the various kinds of hearers who would be listening to their sermons and to think through applications of the truth preached to several different kinds of hearts—hardened sinners, questioning doubters, weary saints, young enthusiasts..."[53] And the list continues.

So think about your listeners and the spiritual condition of their lives. Now, in your sermon application, describe their situation and how the biblical principle of the text should affect them.

Going back to our James 1:19-20 sermon, if you wanted to speak to single mothers, you could say something like this:

---

[53] William Perkins as quoted in Mark Dever and Greg Gilbert, *Preach: Theology Meets Practice* (Nashville: B&H Publishing, 2012), 113.

Maybe you are a single mother. You wake up in the morning, and all you want to do is get the kids dressed, fed, and out the door to school in peace. Is it too much to ask for a morning that doesn't feel like World War III? But the kids complain about their clothes. Their shoes don't feel right. They don't like the breakfast you made. And you've had it with these little demons. But when the rage is about to burst from your mouth, remember: Anger doesn't produce righteousness. Screaming at your kids will not produce righteous kids. So pause for a moment. Lock yourself in the bathroom if you have to. Take a deep breath and ask God to help you keep from saying something that will only cause harm.

Then, you may decide to jump to another segment of your audience: *"Maybe you are at the office, and..."*

At this point, you might object, "My audience is too broad. I cannot possibly speak to everyone like this." You are correct. You can't speak to everyone's exact situation. You don't have enough time. But that's OK. Some applications will cross over. The single mother example above applies to most parents.

People are smart. They will use your examples as inspiration to draw their own conclusions for their specific situation. They may not have kids, but they can see how yelling at a friend or family member doesn't help either.

The Holy Spirit will use your examples to convict people of other things. Don't overestimate your role in the sermon. God will use your effort to speak to people in ways you never imagined. And it will be exactly what they needed to hear.

Jesus, Master Storyteller

Jesus was the master of show, don't tell. After all, he's the greatest preacher of all time. So he used a lot of illustrations.

The Bible tells us that he often spoke in parables (Matthew 13:3). In fact, illustrations account for close to 75 percent of the recorded teachings of Jesus in the Bible.[54]

Jesus' parables were simply earthly stories with heavenly meaning. He knew how to tell a story to communicate a message in a way that did more than entertain his audience.

---

[54]   Bryan Chapell, *Christ-Centered Preaching: Redeeming the Expository Sermon*, Kindle ed. (Grand Rapids: Baker, 2015), Location 4028.

His stories all had a point. But instead of only telling people the point, Jesus chose to show them the point with a parable.

Think about it.

- Jesus could have said, "Love everyone like they are your neighbor." Instead, he told the story of the good Samaritan.

- Jesus could have said, "God wants to save all lost people." Instead, he told the story of the lost sheep.

- Jesus could have said, "Not everyone who hears my words will follow me." Instead, he told the story of the sower.

Jesus used the "show, don't tell" principle. In fact, think about this for a moment. The essence of the incarnation of Christ on the very first Christmas morning was a show, don't tell moment.

God could have continued to tell us what to do. But that wasn't enough. Instead, He broke into earth and became flesh so that He could walk among us. Yes, the ultimate purpose was to atone for the sins of all believers through dying for our sins in our place on the cross. But Jesus also showed us how to live.

His life is a model for us to follow. He is the ultimate example of show, don't tell.

Tips for Telling Stories

If you want to get better at telling stories, here are a few tips to help:

Act it out

Tell the story and re-enact it as if it is happening right now. For example, if you say, "I was walking down the road..." you could walk in place. If you say, "She jumped out and scared me." you could act scared by leaning back, throwing your hands up, and widening your eyes.

Use dialogue

Dialogue makes a story more interesting. Think of the difference betweens saying, "He said he didn't like my preaching." or, "He pointed at my chest and said, 'You are a terrible preacher.'" Which is more interesting?

Use your senses

Add sensory details. In a word or two, describe the look, color, smell, feel, or setting of important elements in a story. Think of the difference between saying, "the ball," and "the red ball." The description evokes a more vivid image in your mind. But be careful, because you can be so descriptive that you clutter the story and bore your audience.

Keep it short

Cut extraneous details. Tell a short story, not a long, drawn-out, bloated novel.

Make a point

Please have a point. It might be a great story, but it's useless without a point. If your story doesn't have a point, delete it.

Check your facts

Fact check all your sources. Check snopes.com if a story sounds too good to be true. Be careful speaking with authority about things in which you're not an expert. And never, ever tell a story if you're not confident of its credibility. You are one Google search away from losing all credibility.

Ask permission

Never poke fun at someone or tell their story without permission. Most sermons today end up on the internet somewhere. Even if you aren't recording it, anyone with a phone could be. So don't tell a story about someone without their permission. At least change their name to protect them.

Don't be a hero

Don't be the hero of your illustrations. Please use stories from your life. Give us a window into how Jesus is impacting your world. Share the surprising, emotional, humorous, painful, or even embarrassing moments from your life. Just remember that humility goes a long way. Even if you tell a story where you did something right, give God credit or thank someone who you couldn't have done it without.

Mental Preparation

Illustrations illuminate a point and prepare us for action. In fact, research has shown that when we rehearse a situation in our mind, it actually helps us perform better in those situations.

Chip and Dan Heath explain that "hearing stories acts as a kind of mental flight simulator, preparing us to respond more quickly and effectively."[55] And your imagination triggers areas of the brain associated with what you imagine:

Brain scans show that when people imagine a flashing light, they activate the visual area of the brain; when they imagine someone tapping on

---

[55]   Chip Heath and Dan Heath, *Made to Stick: Why Some Ideas Survive and Others Die*, Kindle ed. (New York: Random House, 2007), Location 284.

their skin, they activate tactile areas of the brain. The activity of mental simulation is not limited to the insides of our heads. People who imagine words that start with b or p can't resist subtle lip movements, and people who imagine looking at the Eiffel Tower can't resist moving their eyes upward. Mental simulation can even alter visceral physical responses: When people drink water but imagine that it's lemon juice, they salivate more.[56]

In other words, mental practice is almost as good as physical practice. When you tell a story, you mentally prepare your audience for how they should react when they encounter a similar scenario. This means that your illustrations will help people respond better to difficult situations and temptations.

So tell your stories, recreate real-life scenarios, or tell other people's stories. However you do it, be a storyteller. Prepare people for biblical responses to real-life situations.

Don't just tell people what to do; show them how they can do it.

---

[56]   Heath, *Made to Stick*, Location 3354.

ACTION STEP: Walk In Their Shoes

Go through the process of putting yourself in the shoes of a few different segments of your audience (such as parents, students, or office workers). Now, think about how the biblical principle from your sermon applies to them in specific situations. Write your own illustration as detailed and descriptive as possible.

If you are stuck, pick up a phone and call someone you know who is part of that group. They will give you insight into their world that will make your application far better. You could even use your conversation, with their permission, as a story. "I spoke with a young entrepreneur this week who explained to me how this principle changes the way he does business..."

Now, in the application part of your next sermon, ask "so what?" And explain a scenario where this principle can apply to them.

11. HUMOR: Laughter Brings People Together

Laughter is the shortest distance between two people.

— Victor Borge[57]

Laughter is good for the soul.

Think back to a time when you and your friends or family burst into uncontrollable laughter. Aren't these some of the best moments of your life?

---

[57] Victor Borge as quoted in Ken Davis, *Secrets of Dynamic Communications: Prepare with Focus, Deliver with Clarity, Speak with Power* (Nashville: Thomas Nelson, 2013), 125.

Laughter unites us. It reminds us that we are all imperfect. Plus, it feels good.

There are some who argue that there's no place in a sermon for humor—that the message is too serious to be trivialized by jokes. I agree if the pastor isn't funny, or the sermon becomes a standup comedy routine with no biblical teaching. But God created laughter. It was His idea.

Pastors should use God's gift of laughter to communicate God's Word. Plus, there are tremendous benefits of using humor well.

Five Benefits of Humor in a Sermon

1. Humor kills boredom

We worship a God of infinite love, joy, power, wisdom, and creativity. But many sermons do not reflect this.

A boring sermon is not representative of who God is. A dash of humor is one element that can spice up a sermon.

2. Humor grabs attention

A timely joke or funny anecdote has the power to regain the focus of a person whose mind has drifted from the sermon to lunch. When our attention wanders, our ears perk up when people laugh because you want to know what they're laughing about.

3. Humor disarms skeptics

It's impossible to laugh and be angry at the same time. And there are people who come to your church with no intention of liking it.

Maybe they don't believe in "all this nonsense," or they lost trust in organized religion because of a bad experience. So they sit with crossed arms like a barrier to keep anything from getting in. They fully intend to hate your sermon.

But humor can lower these barriers. It has a powerful way of helping uncross arms and open minds.

John Stott says, "We must never joke about serious topics. But humour may be used to break tension, so that people can relax before concentrating again. It may be used to break down people's defences — to move them from stubbornness and rebellion to responsiveness."[58]

4. Humor humanizes you

When pastors joke about themselves, it helps the audience know that they are human. There is a stereo-

[58] John Stott, *The Challenge of Preaching*, Kindle ed. (Cambridge: Wm. B. Eerdmans, 2013), Location 1467.

type that pastors are stuffy, out of touch, and self-righteous. Nothing breaks this stereotype faster than a self-deprecating story.

Also, some things are funny because you say what everyone is thinking, but afraid to say. So if you poke a little harmless fun at odd things that Christian do, you allow people to laugh and know that the pastor has thought the same thing they have.

5. Humor softens hard truth

If you have a potentially harsh word for your audience, humor can be a great way to ease into it.

I know a pastor who is a master at this. He will have the audience rolling on the floor right before he hits them between the eyes with brutal honesty.

For example, he once told a hilarious story about a nagging wife and a man who wished he wasn't married to her. But then he changed his tone and said, "As funny as that is, many of our marriages in this room are on the brink of disaster. And men, you need to stop flirting with thoughts of another woman."

Ouch! But can you imagine if he started with that? What if he jumped right into scolding the men in the room? They would get defensive and stop listening.

Humor helps soften people's hearts and prepare them for moments when you need to tell it like it is.

Christian comedian, Ken Davis, says, "The best definition of humor I have ever heard is this: 'Humor is a gentle way to acknowledge human frailty.' Put another way, humor is a way of saying, 'I'm not okay and you're not okay, but that's okay.' Humor is possible only when people are willing to acknowledge their imperfections. But a skillful communicator who can make an audience laugh (and is able to laugh at himself) opens the door to communicate life-changing information."[59]

Humor leads to agreement about our flaws. It opens the door to honesty about our shortcomings.

What Makes Something Funny?

We know something funny when we see it. But when we are the one trying to be funny, it can be more difficult. Why do some jokes work and others bomb?

Humor is an art, not a science. There is no perfect formula to being funny.

---

[59]   Davis, *Dynamic Communications*, 125.

- Sometimes something is funny because it's unexpected. Sometimes something is funny because we all see it coming.

- Sometimes it's what is said. Other times it's the way it's said.

- Sometimes it's funny because it's true. Sometimes it's funny because it's wildly exaggerated.

As much as I wish I could give you a perfect explanation of how to be funny, like "7 Steps to Hilarious Jokes", humor requires a lot of trial and error.

I've told my fair share of bad jokes. In my head, they were great. But when I delivered them... crickets.

Even the best comedians practice for years and tell a lot of bad jokes before they find what works for them. Fortunately, you are not a comedian. It's easier for preachers to be funny because nobody expects it.

Don't get discouraged if an occasional joke fails, and don't force it because humor can be dangerous.

7 Safeguards for Using Humor in a Sermon

Humor is like a firework. When used the right way, it's a beautiful thing. When used wrong, it can blow up in your face.

Before you go overboard with jokes, try to be a comedian, or say something that gets you in trouble, consider these seven tips:

1. Laugh, then get to the point

The best preachers I know have you rolling one minute and hit you with a hard truth the next. Humor to a preacher is like laughing gas to a dentist; it dulls the pain before the root canal. It softens the blow of painful truth.

Don't allow the joke to hijack the message. Tell it. Laugh about it. Then use it as a short bridge to your big point.

2. Be naturally funny

Be yourself. Use your natural sense of humor. If you are goofy, be goofy. If you are witty, be witty. If you have a dry sense of humor, use dry humor. Please, don't try to be someone you are not. It won't be funny. It won't connect.

Humor has to flow from your natural, God-given personality.

3. Don't preface a joke

Never say things like:

- "This is hilarious..."

- "I heard a really funny story..."

- "You are all going to laugh at me..."

Let the audience decide if it is funny or not. If you set an expectation that something is funny, but nobody laughs, you have set yourself up to fail. If it's funny, people will laugh on their own.

4. Never explain a joke

"Ha ha. Get it? It's funny because..."

If you have to explain a joke, it wasn't funny. Don't tell a joke that only a few people will understand. Explainer jokes often happen when a pastor tells a joke that is funny to their seminary professor, but not their audience.

5. If nobody laughs, keep rolling

If the joke was really bad and nobody laughs, sometimes the best thing you can do is laugh about how bad it was and move on. If you joke about how bad a joke was, you will still get a few laughs.

Later on, you should learn from it. Perform an autopsy on the dead joke. Why did nobody laugh? Was it a bad joke, or just bad delivery? Was it the timing, or maybe the subject of the joke? Was it the wrong audience for that type of joke? Every failure is a learning opportunity.

6. Laugh at yourself

Be self-deprecating. Never laugh at someone else's expense. Some will find it funny; others will think you are a jerk. Plus without intending it, you could embarrass or offend the person you laugh at.

When you poke fun at yourself, people will relate better to you. It's refreshing when a preacher admits they aren't perfect. It grants the audience permission to admit their imperfections too.

7. Don't joke about sensitives subjects

If a joke could even slightly be seen as demeaning towards a person's gender, race, religion, nationality, sexual orientation, or any other sensitive subject, drop it.

You may think it's funny. People might laugh. You may not really mean it. But if people are offended, your joke just got in the way of the gospel. Your inappropriate joke just derailed your sermon, and hurt your credibility. Everything else you say will be forgotten or ignored.

Breaking Barriers

Do people laugh when you preach? And no, I don't mean laughing at you in a bad way because your preaching is so awful. That's the stuff that fills my nightmares. I mean, do people laugh because you intentionally said something funny? Do you use humor as a tool to engage and disarm your listeners?

Try to find one moment in every sermon that you can get a good laugh. You don't have to be a comedian. You shouldn't try to be. You don't have to have the best jokes or any jokes at all. Just have fun. Allow your natural sense of humor to show.

Charles Spurgeon included a lot of humor in his sermons. But some people thought it was too much.

A lady once complained to Spurgeon about his excessive humor. Although she like his preaching and benefited from the content of his messages, she believed his humor was a problem.

Spurgeon listened to her complaint and replied, "Well, madam, you may very well be right; but if you knew the number of jokes I do not tell you, and the number of things that I refrain from saying you would give me more credit than you are giving me."[60] He was a naturally funny guy, so his sermons were naturally humorous. It was part of his God-given personality. And although I cannot prove it, I believe it's one of the reasons his preaching was so effective.

The best preachers know how to get the audience laughing one minute, and listening intensely the next.

Laughter breaks down the walls of hard to reach people and brings them back for more. Laughter eases tension in the room before a few hard words. Plus, it simply makes a sermon more enjoyable to hear.

Laughter is good for the sermon and good for the soul.

ACTION STEP: Watch Funny People

Study a few videos of stand-up comedians and preachers who use humor well. Note how they set up their jokes, and the timing of their delivery.

Now, take what you learned and apply it to your natural sense of humor. Find a moment in your next

---

60   D. Martin Lloyd-Jones, *Preaching and Preachers* (Grand Rapids: Zondervan, 2011), 251.

sermon to insert some humor. It could be a funny story, a quick joke, or pointing out something you find funny about the text.

Don't go overboard, and don't take yourself too seriously. Use your natural sense of humor just as you would in a conversation with friends.

As always, evaluate the audience's response and your delivery. What worked, what didn't work, and how could you do better next time?

12. OBJECTIONS: Speak to Skeptics

Christian communicators must show that they remember (or at least understand) very well what it is like not to believe, all the while maintaining that it is possible to come to real assurance of God's reality and love.

— Tim Keller[61]

Do you remember what it was like to go to church for the first time?

A lot of us have been in church so long that we can't remember. Maybe you grew up going to church

---

[61] Timothy Keller, *Preaching: Communicating Faith in an Age of Skepticism*, Kindle ed. (New York: Penguin, 2015), 84.

with your family like I did. So you were too young to remember.

If you came to faith in Jesus later in life, you might have an advantage in this area. You know how awkward it was. Maybe you didn't know anyone, or you only knew the friend who invited you. Maybe you were nervous, or afraid it would be a cult. However you felt, you were probably more than a bit skeptical.

Whatever your background, try putting yourself in the place of a nonbeliever attending your church for the first time. What are they thinking? What are they feeling? What are they looking for?

If you want to be certain, find someone in your community who doesn't go to church. Ask them to come and give a brutally honest evaluation of their experience. Offer to pay them if you have to.

Ask them to answer questions like: What did you like? What was confusing to you? What was awkward? Was anything intimidating? What was missing? How could it have been a better experience for you? We can't afford to lose touch with what it's like to be a nonbeliever in church if we want to continue to reach people with the good news of Christ.

If your church is trying to reach your community, as it should, then you must assume that skeptics are in the room. Maybe they were invited by a friend, family member, or coworker. Maybe they found your church online. Maybe they had a horrible week and wandered in looking for something, anything to help. You never know who is in the room. So you must be ready to speak to them.

Also, do not be so quick to assume that the people who have sat in your church for years are all believers. I have known many skeptical husbands and wives who go to church out of obligation to their spouse. I have worked with many teenagers go to church because their parents have faith, but they do not.

Here's the bottom line: If you want to reach people with the gospel, you need to speak to them.

If you want unchurched people to visit your church and love it, you need to talk to them. Acknowledge that they are in the room. Let them know you are thinking about them. Eliminate as many barriers and objections getting in the way between them and God as possible. Help them feel like your church is a safe place for them to explore and ask questions.

Your preaching will be a determining factor in whether unchurched people return. Regardless of whether they like the music, programs, or people in your church, the sermon will either compel them or repel them. It will draw them in or push them away.

So the question must be asked: Does your preaching produce a desire in skeptics to want to come back to hear more?

We have an obligation to defend our beliefs both to challenge the doubts of skeptics and to build the faith of believers.

We see this mandate in 1 Peter 3:15, when Peter writes, "Always be prepared to give an answer to everyone who asks you to give the reason for the hope that you have."[62] This command ought to apply to our preaching as much as every other area of our lives. As R.C. Sproul says, "Defending the faith to the best of our ability is not a luxury or an indulgence in intellectual vanity. It is the task given to each one of us as we bear witness to our faith before the world."[63]

---

[62] 1 Peter 3:15 NIV

[63] R.C. Sproul, *Defending Your Faith: An Introduction* (Wheaton: Crossway, 2003), 10.

Four Reasons You Should Address Skeptics in Every Sermon

There may be others, but I can think of four significant benefits of speaking to skeptics in every sermon.

1. Speaking to skeptics reaches skeptics

This is the most obvious benefit. If you want to reach skeptics, you have to talk to them. When you lovingly address their doubts and concerns, you show that you understand what they are thinking. As a result, they will be more receptive to hear what you have to say. There will be fewer barriers between them and the gospel.

2. Speaking to skeptics encourages people to invite skeptical friends

If you have ever invited a friend to church, you know that your perspective of the service changes. You begin to see everything from your friend's point of view. You cringe if things are awkward, and if the pastor talks only to insiders.

Afterward, you may apologize and make a few excuses, hoping they will give church another chance. And you may hesitate when inviting people to your church again because you are embarrassed about what they might experience.

When churches fail to speak to unbelievers in the room, people stop inviting unbelievers. However, when a church speaks to unbelievers every week, people are confident that they can invite them. They know they aren't bringing an outsider to a members-only meeting.

3. Speaking to the skeptics teaches people how to speak to skeptics

Your people will hear how you answer and explain a skeptic's doubts and objections to Christianity. You may not realize it, but you are equipping your church to repeat what they learn to their friends. By listening to you share your faith, they are learning how to share theirs. Therefore, preaching to skeptics becomes part of the discipleship and evangelism strategy of your church. You are training people how to respond to difficult questions.

4. Speaking to skeptics strengthens the faith of your church

We all wrestle with doubt at times. Don't forget that the skeptics are sometimes people who have been attending your church for a long time. They may have never fully believed, or they may be in a season of doubt. Addressing common doubts and misconceptions will build the faith of both newcomers and longtime members.

Answering Objections

Some people object to this style of preaching. The most common complaints I hear about preaching this way is that it waters down the message, it ignores the discipleship of faithful Christians, and it turns every sermon into an apologetics lesson. Let's think about this:

1. Speaking to skeptics does not mean watering down the message

You don't have to dumb down a message to talk to unbelievers. In fact, it requires more depth of study. You've got to know your stuff if you're going to answer tough questions in a way that everyone can understand. And when you address common objections, you add a layer of depth to the message that makes people engage in critical thinking.

2. Speaking to skeptics does not mean that you do not also speak to long-time church members

I've mentioned this already. Don't assume that everyone in the room who identifies as a Christian is one. And for those who are mature believers, remember that you are modeling for them how to share their faith, and creating an environment where they can confidently invite unbelievers to visit.

3. Speaking to skeptics does not mean that every sermon is an apologetics lesson

Addressing common misconceptions and doubts doesn't need to take the entire message. You may just add a few facts, acknowledge the weird stuff in the Bible, answer a few questions, defend your logic, provide further resources for people with more questions, or let them know they are welcome to ask you questions after the service.

Tips For Preaching To Skeptics

Entire books are written about the many details and nuances of preaching to skeptics. Unfortunately, there's not enough room to cover it all here. So start with these five tips:

1. Be interesting

One of the first objections people have to church is that it's boring. They think it is irrelevant, outdated, and a waste of time. The best way to shatter this stereotype is to work hard to be a better preacher.

Write a great message and follow the principles in this book to preach a more engaging, interesting, humorous, memorable, authentic, and compelling sermon. Just remember, you cannot do it all on your own. Apart from the grace of God and the power of the Holy Spirit working through you, you can do nothing. So practice these principles, but rely on God's power to save.

2. Acknowledge them

One of the best ways to talk to skeptics is to let them know that you know they're in the room.

You may decide to welcome them in the introduction. It could be as simple as saying something like, "If you are new here and don't know if you believe this whole Jesus thing, that's OK. We are glad you are here."

You may want to talk to them in the application. Saying something like, "Maybe you are here today, and you don't know if you buy all this. OK. That's fair. But what if it's true? Maybe you have resisted this for far too long. I would simply ask, how has that been working for you?"

Don't talk to skeptics the same way in every sermon. The key is to find parts of your message where it's a natural fit to acknowledge that they are in the room. Let them know they are welcome in your church, and that it's a safe place for them to question, doubt, and search for answers.

3. Lead with gentleness and respect

At the beginning of the chapter, I quoted 1 Peter 3:15, "Always be prepared to give an answer to everyone who asks you to give the reason for the hope that you have." Most Christians know this piece of the Bible and are ready to defend their faith. But many of us ignore the next verse.

Peter continues, "But do this with *gentleness and respect*, keeping a clear conscience, so that those who speak maliciously against your good behavior in Christ may be ashamed of their slander."[64]

We must speak to skeptics with gentleness and respect. I've never met someone who was won to Christ in a shouting match. When people yell at you, you become defensive. The walls come up, and nothing gets through.

When we attack skeptics and nonbelievers, we destroy our credibility. Even if they question our beliefs, we should hold ourselves to such a high standard that they cannot deny our character.

So please, in your life and your preaching, don't try to demoralize and attack skeptics. People need to know that you care about them—that you want something for them, not from them. Skeptics are wondering if you just want their money, or more butts in seats to pad your ego. So speak the truth in love (Ephesians 4:15).

Tim Keller says it well: "The Christian preacher must be a critic of nonbelief. However, there is no virtue in being an unsympathetic one. Do doubters come away feeling you are indifferent, high-handed, or dismissive of their views, or are they surprised, even shocked at how accurately and fairly you repre-

---

[64]   1 Peter 3:15-16 NIV emphasis added.

sent their own problems with Christianity? Do they think that you can express their skeptical views as well as—or even better than—they can themselves?"[65]

4. Argue with yourself

One of the most effective ways I have seen to address skeptics is to argue with yourself in the sermon.

After you make a point, ask yourself a critical question that some people in the audience are probably thinking. Say things like:

- "OK, Brandon, come on. You don't really believe that do you?"

- "Hold on. How can you say that when...?"

- "But what about...?"

As you study and prepare your message, keep skeptics in mind. Object to controversial elements in your sermon before they do. Then, you can give a thoughtful response to their objections.

5. Recognize the unbelievable things in the Bible

We must admit that there are weird and unbelievable things in the Bible that are outside the realm of

---

[65]   Keller, *Preaching*, 84.

common experience. We read about things like a talking snake, a worldwide flood, the parting of the Red Sea, Jesus walking on water, dead people coming back to life, and more. I think we can all agree that these things are not normal.

So be on the lookout for what Keller calls "defeaters":

> These are ideas that, if accepted, make one think, *If this is true, then Christianity can't be true.* Common defeaters include "There can't be just one way to God"; "We can't believe in a God who sends people to hell"; "Science has disproven the supernatural"; and "The Bible has many offensive, outdated parts that we can no longer accept."[66]

Anytime we teach on a passage that contains something that's hard to believe, we would be foolish not to pause to acknowledge that what we just read is not normal, and then offer a simple reason to why we believe it. Here are a few examples of what this might sound like:

- You may be thinking, "That's not normal." And you're right. It's not normal. But Jesus is not a

---

66   Keller, *Preaching*, 85.

normal human being. If Jesus really is the Son of God (which he said he was), and he really did die and rise from the dead (which I believe he did), then why couldn't he heal a sick person?

- "But isn't that impossible? What about science?" Well, if God is real and He created the universe (which includes all the laws of science that govern it), might it be possible that He, knowing infinitely more than we have discovered, could apply the laws of science in ways we cannot yet fully understand. After all, what we know about science is continually growing and adapting because we only know a fraction of all there is to know about the universe. If you could travel back in time only 100 years and tell people what we can do with technology today, they too would say, "That's impossible!"

Your response may not completely resolve their doubt, but at least it shows that you are not a fool, blindly following some mystical tail. You are an intelligent person who has thought deeply about these things.

Andy Stanley says, "As a general rule, say what you suspect unbelievers are thinking. When you do, it gives you credibility. And it gives them space. It says you are a rational being like they are, that you didn't check your brain at the door and you don't expect them to either."[67]

If you need help responding to questions about miracles or other "defeaters" there are plenty of great apologetics books that you can reference.

Find the Fly

I love what Gregory Koukl says in his book, *Tactics*: "If Christianity is the truth, no matter how convincing the other side sounds at first, there will always be a fly in the ointment somewhere — a mistake in thinking, a wayward 'fact,' an unjustified conclusion. Keep looking for it. Sooner or later it will show up."[68] As you prepare to preach to skeptics, find that hole in their thinking.

Much more could be said about preaching to skeptics, but the main point is this: If you want to

---

67   Andy Stanley, *Deep and Wide: Creating Churches Unchurched People Love to Attend* (Grand Rapids: Zondervan, 2012), 252.

68   Gregory Koukl, *Tactics: A Game Plan for Discussing Your Christian Convictions* (Grand Rapids: Zondervan, 2009), 28.

reach people with the gospel, you need to talk to them. As Paul said, "Faith comes from hearing" (Romans 10:17).

ACTION STEP: Listen to a Skeptic

You cannot speak well to skeptics if you do not know any. So go have an honest conversation with a person who is skeptical of Christianity.

If you don't know a single skeptic, ask people in your church if they can refer you to someone. You could also join a Facebook group for your community and extend an invitation to buy anyone a cup of coffee if they would be willing to help you understand their doubts about Christianity.

The goal of this exercise is not to argue with the person. Your goal is to ask questions, shut your mouth, and listen. Seek first to understand their thinking so you can learn how to respond to their objections.

13. NOTES: Less Is More

If you sweat in the study, you can relax in the pulpit. You may not remember every quote, reference, or list, but you can preach with confidence when you know the meaning and message of the text.

— H.B. Charles Jr.[69]

Growing up, I never wanted to be a pastor because public speaking scared me to death.

If I were to have ranked my worst fears in order, it would have been:

---

[69]   H.B. Charles Jr., *On Preaching: Personal & Pastoral Insights for the Preparation & Practice of Preaching*, Kindle ed. (Chicago: Moody, 2014), Location 1179.

1. Girls

2. Public speaking

3. Death

I started in ministry as a worship leader. In middle school and high school, I led my youth group in worship twice a week. It wasn't always good, but somebody had to do it.

I would stand in front of the group, acoustic guitar in hand, with a music stand in front of me and lead worship while staring at the notes the whole time. I never looked up. I never moved around. The notes had my undivided attention.

My first sermon was a lot like my early days leading worship. I hid behind the biggest podium I could find, clutching my notes in both hands.

My sermon notes, like my worship notes, were my lifeline. I never took my eyes off them. I was afraid that if I did, I would miss something important and crash the sermon.

It wasn't until I was in college and served in the band of a large church that a veteran worship pastor told me I had to ditch the music stand.

I panicked. What if I play the wrong chords? What if I forget the lyrics? I am not good at memorizing music. I'm going to fail! Everyone will laugh at me!

But the worship pastor didn't give me a choice. And I'm glad he didn't.

Ditching the music stand forced me to memorize the songs. It wasn't as hard as I thought. It made me look up at the audience. And it freed me to worship God without worrying about what was coming next. My performance improved, and I was more authentic in my worship.

That music stand that I thought I desperately needed was a crutch holding me back from reaching my full potential as a worship leader.

Fast forward a few years, and someone else challenged me to preach without notes. It was one of the scariest things I ever did, but like my experience with leading worship, my sermon delivery improved considerably. And the more I practiced, the better I got.

Many preachers are tied to their podium by their notes like I was to my music stand. They think their notes are a tool to help them, but in reality, it's holding them back from reaching their full potential.

Bryan Chapell says that "preachers greatly err when they think that by reading every word precisely as written they have better communicated. Far better to stumble over a phrase, smile confidently, and correct it than to speak perfectly while displaying the top of your head as you read the bulk of the sermon."[70]

Believe it or not, reducing your notes or eliminating them altogether will force you to internalize the message, improving your delivery.

The Point

Just like throwing out your music stand helps your worship, throwing out your notes (or using fewer notes) helps your preaching. This doesn't mean you prepare any less. In fact, memorizing a song takes more time than reading music. Likewise, preaching without notes takes more preparation because you have no safety net.

Now, if the thought of preaching without notes terrifies you, then you have proven my point. You are too dependent on your notes. You don't know what to do without them.

Don't believe me? I triple dog dare you to give it a shot. What do you have to lose? You might preach a

---

[70] Bryan Chapell, *Christ-Centered Preaching: Redeeming the Expository Sermon*, Kindle ed. (Grand Rapids: Baker, 2015), Location 7513.

bad sermon. Or you may just preach your best sermon yet.

The risk is low compared to the benefits you could gain.

7 Benefits of Preaching Without Notes (Or Just a Few Notes)

1. You will preach more from your heart

Even if you write a sermon from the heart, you communicate the opposite when you have to look down to find what to say next.

What would you find to be more sincere: if I wrote you an apology email, or if I were to look you in the eyes and tell you how sorry I am?

The written word is powerful, but it cannot fully capture the heart. In the same way, your notes can get in the way of fully communicating what God has laid on your heart.

2. You will sound more conversational

You will sound more natural and less rehearsed—more like a preacher and less like a politician.

When you preach without notes, you will preach similar to how you talk to people. You will use more of the words that you use in a normal conversation. Your true personality will come through.

Reading notes, or even looking at them too often looks and feels more formal. It's how politicians give speeches.

3. You will have more eye contact with your audience

As we discussed in chapter 3, eye contact is incredibly important. Research shows that good eye contact builds trust, shows confidence, increases engagement, and helps you read your audience.

You can't look at your notes and your audience at the same time. Even if you could, you would look way cross-eyed.

4. You will be able to move around the stage

When you are reliant on notes, you are stuck behind a podium. Plus, podiums create a barrier between you and the audience. Without notes, you are free to make more use of the space on the stage. Good movement on stage will increase your audience's attention.

You will have the option to remove the podium altogether if you want or use a smaller stand or table off to the side for your Bible and a few notes.

5. You will have to be more prepared

For me, preaching from my notes was lazy. Once I put in the hard work of writing my message, I wanted to stop. It was much easier to read what I wrote than to put in the extra effort to internalize the message. Preaching without notes forced me to prepare more.

Most pastors are afraid to ditch their notes because they are afraid they will miss a point. But you have to realize that nobody will know if you do. Your audience has no idea what you planned to say. You are the only person who will know. Plus, this fear of missing something will drive you to prepare better.

6. You will allow more room for the Holy Spirit

Have you ever had a moment where God brings something to mind in the midst of preaching that you hadn't thought of before?

Often those little thoughts the Holy Spirit gives me are the most powerful point in the entire sermon. If I were tied to my notes, I would likely stick to the script. Freeing myself from notes allows the flexibility for those Holy Spirit moments.

As Charles Spurgeon said, "Anything is better than mechanical sermonizing, in which the direction of the Spirit is practically ignored."[71]

7. You will use better gestures

Your body follows your focus. The more you focus on your notes, the more your body wants to focus on them as well.

Your head angle downward, you will stand close to the notes, and your hands will want to touch or rest next to the page as you read. Your gestures likely consist of lifting your hands off the podium and setting them down again.

But when you focus less on reading your message, your are free to focus on the delivery.

How I Use Notes

I still write a full sermon manuscript to clarify my thoughts, because I often don't know what I think about something until I write it down. But I only allow myself to bring a single page of notes with me on stage.

---

[71] Charles H. Spurgeon, *Lectures To My Students* (Fig, 2012), 92.

Most of the notes are direct quotes of the Scripture passages I am teaching because I want to read these word-for-word so I don't make any mistakes with God's Word. I like to have a Bible with me, but I print the Scripture because I don't want to waste time or get lost trying to flip through the thin pages to find the exact chapter and verse.

The rest of my notes are a brief outline with a few key points and reminders of illustrations that I don't want to forget.

(To see an example of my notes go to www.Pro-Preacher.com/Deliver.)

Sure, there are plenty of good preachers who use a lot of notes. There are some who can get away with reading from a full manuscript. But I believe the best, most engaging preachers rarely rely on their notes.

You may be wondering, "But how do you actually go about preaching without notes? Isn't it hard? Isn't it risky? What if I don't have a great memory?"

As scary as preaching without notes sounds, the great news is that you can preach with little to no notes. You have the ability. Don't believe the self-defeating lie that you can't.

Our brains are a wonderful gift from God. Like a muscle, the more you exercise it, the stronger it gets.

It may be difficult at first, but the more you preach without notes, the more your brain will adapt. It will get easier over time. Your ability to retain and recall your sermon will grow. It just takes practice.

To get started, follow these three simple steps:

1. Absorb the text

Preaching without notes does not equate to a lack of preparation. In fact, you need to prepare more to do it well.

Approach your study like a sponge. Absorb the primary passage of Scripture so much that it leaks out of you.

Read it over and over again. Take notes of everything you observe. Ask questions. Find answers. Read commentaries. By the time you finish, you should be an expert on the text.

You need to know the text so well that if all you had in your hand was a Bible, you could almost fill the entire sermon time just talking about it.

2. Memorize thoughts, not words

You are not an actor reciting lines. You are a preacher communicating God's truth. If you forget a few words or an illustration, nobody will know. It's OK.

You are only in trouble if you forget the outline. Even if you don't bring it with you on stage, you still need an outline. Focus your memorization on the outline. Think of your sermon as blocks of thought. Memorize thought-for-thought, not word-for-word.

As I mentioned earlier, write a full manuscript of your message (or at least a highly detailed outline) to organize your thoughts. Writing the sermon is vital. Because, as John Stott says, "Few people are such clear thinkers and talkers that they can express themselves well without written preparation."[72]

Copy your manuscript into a new document, and cut it down to a single page. Fitting your message on one page forces you to keep only the most important thoughts. This page is your outline. The more simple your outline, the better. It's a lot harder to memorize a 15 point sermon than a 3 pointer—or better yet, a one point message.

I also find that using the same outline format for each sermon helps you remember your sermon easier.

---

[72]   John Stott, *The Challenge of Preaching*, Kindle ed. (Cambridge: Wm. B. Eerdmans, 2013), Location 1239.

3. Rehearse, rehearse, rehearse

To preach without notes well, you have to know your message cold. The final step is to rehearse your message out loud.

The night before preaching, I read my manuscript out loud a few times. Then I try to deliver the message without looking it. I only look at the pages when I draw a blank on the next thought. Finally, I rehearse my entire message without looking at all.

On Sunday morning, I talk through the outline in the shower and on my drive to church. By the time I stand on stage, I have absorbed my message so much that I cannot wait to let it out.

I never preach the manuscript word for word. But after going through this process, I'm always amazed how natural it is to preach the same sermon in multiple services with only slight differences in each message.

I have gone into much further detail on my studying, writing, outlining, and rehearsal process in my book, *Preaching Nuts & Bolts*. So check it out if you want more ideas and time-saving tips on sermon preparation.

You Can Do It

Preaching without notes may sound terrifying to you. It used to scare me too. But you can do this! You have it in you. God has gifted you with a powerful brain that only needs a little practice.

You don't need an exceptional memory. You just have to put in the work. And like everything else, the more you do it, the better you will get.

Freeing yourself from your notes may be what you need to take your preaching to the next level. So give it a shot.

Don't get discouraged if you're not perfect at first. Take Martyn Lloyd-Jones' advice: "Do not be too downcast if you happen to have a very bad service and say that you will never again enter a pulpit without a fully written sermon lying on the desk before you. That is the voice of the devil. Do not listen to him; go on until you arrive at a stage where you know that you are free."[73]

---

[73] D. Martin Lloyd-Jones, *Preaching and Preachers* (Grand Rapids: Zondervan, 2011), 241.

ACTION STEP: Write a One Page Outline

Create a simple one-page outline of your next sermon using the tips from this chapter. Then, memorize the outline so you can know each thought without looking at anything but Scripture. Now, if you are brave, bring nothing but a Bible with you to preach it. If that's too scary, you can do what I do and bring only the one-page outline.

Afterward, evaluate how it went. How did you do? Did you forget anything major? How did the audience respond? Did you feel more connected or more conversational in your delivery? Was your outline too complicated? What should you do next time to continue to improve?

14. TECHNOLOGY: Gain Clarity, Lose Distractions

We must trust God, not our computers, projectors and amplifiers (all of which can crash or lead us into temptation). We should thank God for technology, but not rely on it.

— *John Stott*[74]

In the grand scheme of Christian history, modern technology is still a recent addition. Not too long ago pastors did not have the luxury of sound systems, microphones, or projectors.

---

[74]   John Stott, *The Challenge of Preaching*, Kindle ed. (Cambridge: Wm. B. Eerdmans, 2013), Location 219.

It's hard to imagine what it would have been like to preach to large crowds in those days. While trying to project so all could hear, the strain on your voice must have been unbearable at times. Most pastors had a limit to how many people they could speak to because their voices would not carry far enough.

There were a few exceptions. George Whitefield, the 18th-century evangelist, had such a powerful voice that he was able to preach in the open air to crowds of up to twenty-five thousand people.

In fact, Benjamin Franklin wrote in his autobiography about how he believed the rumors of Whitefield's voice to be impossible. So, being the scientific man that he was, Franklin performed an experiment. He went to listen to Whitfeield preach and found that Whitefield was able to be heard over 500 feet away. Much to Franklin's surprise, after doing the math and allowing two square feet per person in a semi-circle, he found the rumors were indeed true! In fact, Franklin calculated that Whitefield could even be heard by more than thirty thousand people.[75] Wow! That man truly had a booming voice.

---

[75] Benjamin Franklin, *The Autobiography of Benjamin Franklin* (Boston: Houghton, Mifflin and Company, 1888), 135.

Fortunately today, we don't all have to possess the lungs of Whitefield. We have microphones and powerful sound systems. Everyone can hear us with little vocal strain. We also have audio and video recording capabilities so people no longer even have to be in the room to hear us preach. Anyone, anywhere, at anytime can hear our sermons if we post them online.

But while modern technology is a powerful tool, it can also make things more complicated. Technology is always changing. Entire books could be written on the best use of technology in preaching, but they would be outdated within a year.

In this chapter, I will get into a few details. But I only have the time to touch the surface. My goal is not to answer all your technical questions. You would be better served to do a quick search on the internet if you want the most relevant technology tips. Instead, we will focus primarily on a few fundamentals.

The Golden Rule of Church Technology

The single, overarching principle for technology in preaching is this: technology should add clarity, not distraction.

We've all seen what happens when technology fails. Maybe you were preaching your guts out. The audience was leaning in. God was moving. Then, it happened. Faulty technology spoiled a great sermon.

It could have been many things:

- Feedback in the speakers.

- Popping sounds from the microphone.

- The microphone battery died.

- The projector inexplicably shut off.

- The building lost power.

- The worship team's new smoke machines triggered the fire alarms.

Yes, all these and more have happened to me, and the list could go on.

I once preached a sermon that I thought was one of my best yet. But I was horrified watching the recording. My mic popped and hissed throughout the entire message. It was distracting and embarrassing because I didn't even realize it.

How many times has something like this happened to you?

When technology is at its best, it's invisible, because it's simply a tool to help deliver a clear message. But when technology is bad, it's obvious. It distracts the audience and derails a good sermon.

Audio, lighting, and video are all tools to aid the clarity of the presentation. If at any time they become a distraction from God, either fix it or eliminate it.

Microphones

Today we have many options for preaching microphones. So when considering what microphone to use, you need to remember the primary technology principle and ask this question: Which microphone will help me preach with clarity while limiting distractions?

Think about this question while we explore some options available today.

Podium mic

The podium mic is the most dated microphone for preaching. As its name suggest, this microphone is attached to the podium.

It can be useful for situations where multiple people will speak from a podium, such as a funeral or commencement ceremony. However, it's often visible in front of the preacher. It chains the pastor to the podium because sound decreases the further away they move. And if the pastor is not holding in the same spot, head pointing towards the microphone, the volume level fluctuates.

If you want a more academic or traditional feel to your sermon and you preach directly from a manuscript, this mic may be your preference. Otherwise, I recommend choosing a different option.

Wireless lavalier mic

Lavalier microphones (also called lapel microphones) were popular in churches years ago because they offered a handsfree, less visible, wireless option.

These are the microphones that clip onto your clothing, typically on the lapel of a suit, or the edge of a tie or button-up shirt. You may notice that a lot of TV talk shows today use this kind of microphone.

Unfortunately, lavalier microphones are not ideal for on-stage speaking environments. They are much easier to control in a small television studio than in a live stage setting like a church or concert. Because of where the microphone clips, they are often too far away from the preacher's mouth. This causes the need to increase the volume level, which can result in picking up feedback and excess room noise.

Most churches have moved on from lavalier microphones because it's hard to get the sound level right. You may find that this works for you, but I think there are better options.

Wireless handheld mic

Some pastors prefer a wireless handheld microphone. A handheld microphone offers flexibility for the pastor to control their volume by holding the mic closer to their mouth or further away. It works well for eccentric preachers who love to move from shouts to whispers.

Sound techs, however, often don't like handheld microphones precisely because the pastor has too much control. The tech cannot control a consistent volume level. If the pastor is holding the mic too far away, the tech will have to boost the volume and risk feedback. If the pastor brings the mic too close, they will have to lower the volume, so it isn't too loud for the audience. In addition, handheld microphones limit your gestures since one hand is always holding the mic.

I love this mic for other people on the platform— worship, announcements, offering talks, communion talk, or interviews. It is a natural mic for people to understand, pass around, and feel comfortable with.

You may choose this microphone because it's simple and provides you with more control. But it adds too much for the sound team and me to worry about. So I prefer a handheld microphone as a backup or as the next best option.

Wireless headset

The headset mic is the most popular choice for preachers today. Sound techs like them because they offer clearer, fuller, and more controlled sound since they are positioned near the speaker's mouth. Pastors like them because they're hands free, wireless, and deliver quality sound. So this is the option I use and recommend the most.

But, as with all technology, there is still the potential for distractions that you need to beware.

My biggest struggle with a headset mic is that I move a lot. If not fit properly, the mic can wiggle and fall off my ear, drift from my mouth, or get too close. If not positioned correctly, I can also get unwanted wind from breathing and plosives—the puff of air sound caused when making "p" sounds. Also, I've known pastors with beards who have trouble with the mic rubbing their beard, making scratching sounds.

Therefore, as good as this microphone is, it's not for everyone. Find the microphone that works best for you to add clarity and eliminate distraction.

(For my recommendations on the best mics go to www.ProPreacher.com/Deliver)

Mic Tips

Your microphone is one of your most essential tools. You will likely use one every time you preach, so you need to learn some best practices. To ensure limited distraction, here are a few tips you should consider:

- Have a backup wireless mic, just in case. It's faster to switch than changing the batteries while everyone stares at you.

- Use new batteries every week. If you're using rechargeable batteries to save money, change them before every service.

- Have an extra headset cable, just in case. In my experience, the cable that runs from a headset microphone down your back to the wireless battery pack is the first thing to break.

- Adjust the mic and do a sound check on stage before the service. Then, don't touch it unless there's a noticeable problem.

- If you have trouble with a headset microphone moving around on your ear, try using some clear, first aid tape behind your ear to help secure it in place.

Finally, when a mic goes bad, pause and acknowledge it. Apologize. Joke about it. Fix it fast. Then, move on.

I was at a conference recently listening to a nationally renowned preacher. In the middle of his talk, he knocked the headset mic off his ear. It was a distraction, but he handled it beautifully. He paused, fiddled with it for a moment, and quickly recovered by joking, "Whoops. I got a little too excited." Everyone laughed, and he jumped right back into his message.

Don't let the microphone get in the way of the message. Your sermon is too important to be derailed by technical difficulties. Take necessary precautions, train your volunteers, test everything, and invest in the right equipment.

Lighting

Pastors don't often think about lighting, but it's important. If the stage is too dark, people will not be able to see your face. People will be less engaged with your expressions, and more likely to get sleepy.

Calvin Miller says the worst thing about poorly lit preaching is that "people need to be able to see the passion, the body language, and the drama of what they attend. Great words spoken in darkness quickly become invisible as well as inaudible."[76]

A sermon is most effective when the preacher's face and eyes are visible. Therefore, to add clarity and eliminate distractions, there are a few principles you need to know about lighting.

Many churches make the mistake of having lights directly over the preacher's head. But lights over the pastor's head cast shadows on their face under the eye sockets and nose. So their face is dark, and their eyes are hidden from the audience. The same effect can also come from spotlights in front of the stage at too high of an angle.

Some churches remedy this problem with a direct spotlight in the preacher's eyes. It provides a well-lit

---

[76] Calvin Miller, *Preaching: The Art of Narrative Exposition* (Grand Rapids: Baker, 2006), 192.

face and the reflection of light you want to see in their eyes. But although this looks great to the audience, you don't want to blind the pastor. Direct spotlights can be painful.

So the ideal setup has two lights, one to the left and one to the right side of the preacher at a 45-degree angle. It's easier on the eyes and allows the light to be fixed at a lower angle without blinding them. And you still get a well-lit face and a glimmer of light in the pastor's eyes.

Aside from the stage lights, you also need to think about the house lights—the lights shining on the audience. Many worship leaders like the house lights dimmed while singing. But preaching is different.

You want to see the faces of your audience so you can read them and make eye contact. It also allows people to see while taking notes, following along in their Bible, or using a Bible app on their phone without distracting everyone with the glow of the screen. So find a good level to bring up the house lights during your sermon.

Video

Years ago, I was a pastor at a large, multi-site church in New Mexico. We had a movie-theater-sized screen behind the pastor that displayed the sermon series art that our graphic design team created.

Normally, it was great. It set the mood for the series and provided a backdrop to the sermon video that we sent to our video campuses. But one week we were in a series that had an underwater theme. The design team had outdone themselves creating a computer-animated, moving, underwater scene. Picture the landscape from the movie *Finding Nemo*. It was beautiful.

Unfortunately, the video became a big distraction. A large, orange fish swam endlessly around and behind the preacher's head. I'm sure the sermon was great, but I only remember the fish.

Video screens are now common in churches. They used to be rare, but as technology has improved and prices have decreased, they're almost expected. They are a powerful tool for illustrating your sermon with Bible verses, pictures, sermon graphics, and videos. But as wonderful as screens are, like all technology, they can either add clarity to your message or be a huge distraction.

Once again, you need to apply the primary technology principle. In everything you put on the screens, ask: does this add clarity or distraction?

Also, here are a few more tips:

Keep each slide simple

Cluttered slides add distraction. Don't display the entire outline or multiple points at a time. Keep each slide to a single point or image.

Use quality images

Dated, poorly designed, or low-resolution images are a distraction. You would be better using nothing at all.

If you don't have a good eye for design, get help. There are tons of online resources available to help. You may also have graphic artists, video editors, or photographers in your church that could help.

Follow copyright laws

You need to be aware of copyright laws. In general, if you do not own the rights to an image, video, or song, you could be breaking the law if you show them without permission. Doing a quick online search will help you with everything you need to know about current church copyright laws.

Clarity, Not Distraction

If you have more technical questions about church audio, video, or lighting, there are many great websites and church technology experts that would be better suited to help you with technical questions.

Concerning your preaching, I simply want you to remember and apply the number one principle for technology: Technology should add clarity, not distraction.

Do everything you can to present a clear message using the technology available to you, but do not allow it to become a distraction.

Think ahead about all the things that could go wrong with your technology and have safeguards and backup procedures in place for when it fails you.

And don't allow yourself to get distracted by all the lights and buttons of the latest gizmo. At the end of the day, technology is simply a tool to help you present the gospel more clearly.

ACTION STEP: Check Your Tech

Evaluate the technology in your church based on the number one technology principle. Does it add clarity or distraction? Then start making the necessary changes.

- **AUDIO**: Are you using the optimal preaching microphone? Do you have a backup plan for when your batteries die or the mic breaks? What distractions have you had recently, and how could you avoid them?

- **LIGHTING**: Have someone stand on the stage under your lights. Are they well lit? Are there any shadows on their face? Can you see the light reflecting off their eyes? Are they blinded? Are the house lights at a proper level, so they see the faces in the audience? Are they washed out by the stage background?

- **VIDEO**: Look at your recent slides, images, and videos. Are they professional looking, or dated? Are they beautiful or ugly? Are they simple, or too cluttered? Do they add clarity or distraction?

15. APPEARANCE: Look Like Your Audience

The Father made your body, Jesus paid for your body, the Spirit lives in your body. You better take care of it.

— Rick Warren[77]

This chapter is superficial. Let's just get that out of the way. You may be quick to dismiss outward appearance and skip this section, but don't be too hasty.

[77] Madison Park, "Rick Warren and church tackle obesity." Cited 20 February 2017. Online: http://www.cnn.com/2012/01/24/health/saddleback-warren-diet/

Like it or not, before you ever say a word, your appearance says something to the audience.

Before you get the wrong idea, please understand that I don't think that pastors should become vain, fashionistas always obsessing over their looks in the mirror. But we would be foolish to think that appearance doesn't matter.

We ought to at least consider our outward appearance and what it might communicate to the audience. In fact, as much as you may like to think looks don't matter, you don't really believe it. Let me prove it to you.

If looks don't matter, then, when you wake up for church this weekend don't get dressed, don't do your hair, and don't wear any shoes. Just go preach in whatever you slept in the night before.

If you got uncomfortable just thinking about that, then you proved my point. If appearance doesn't matter, then why do clothes matter so much to you?

Looks do matter. They're not everything. They're not the most important thing. But looks do matter at some level. If you are like me, you've even had nightmares about preaching in your underwear. So please don't say that appearance doesn't matter at all because we all know that there are certain cultural standards of appearance that do matter.

To a certain extent, your appearance matters. So let's talk a little superficial.

What Should You Wear?

Paul gives his philosophy for trying to reach various people groups when he said, "I have become all things to all people, that by all means I might save some. I do it all for the sake of the gospel, that I may share with them in its blessings" (1 Corinthians 9:22-23 ESV). Put simply; you need to relate to people, so they are more receptive to hear you share the gospel.

We could apply this verse many ways, but one application is in how we dress when preaching. People relate more to people who dress like they do. So if you were a missionary in a foreign land, you would try to dress more like the people you are trying to reach. Can you imagine trying to reach an indigenous tribe in the Amazon while wearing a three-piece Armani suit?

If you feel the urge to reject what I'm saying here, be careful. Rather than trying to rebel against cultural standards of dress, if you want to reach a culture, you need to observe their standards.

You should study your community. Who are the people you are trying to reach, and how do they tend to dress?

If you are preaching to teenagers, you want to dress more like a high schooler. If you are preaching to silver-haired adults, you want to dress more like a senior adult. If you are preaching in an inner-city church, you want to dress more like people in that city. If you are preaching in a country church, you want to dress more like people in the country. You get the point.

This doesn't mean you should go overboard. You don't have to start reading fashion magazines and follow every latest trend. Don't be a fake. And never dress in a way that compromises your morals.

But you should adapt your style as best as you can to fit your culture. If you preach in a culture where everyone shows up in a suit and tie, you should wear something formal. If you preach in a culture where everyone wears flip-flops and t-shirts, you should wear something casual.

Clothing Tips

For your best appearance on stage, consider the following tips.

- **Dress for your audience.** Tailor your outfit to the people you are trying to reach.

- **Keep the focus on God.** Don't draw too much attention to yourself. Anything that is too flashy, odd, tight, or revealing can distract people from focusing on Jesus.

- **Look clean.** Whatever style of clothing you wear, avoid anything with bad stains and wrinkles. The type-A people will be distracted by how much they want to spray you with stain remover and hit you with an iron.

- **Shower.** People may not be close enough to smell you on stage, but they will be before and after the service. Take a shower before leaving home, so you look, feel, and smell clean.

- **Dress above average.** If you're not sure what to wear, dress slightly above the average person in your audience. This is a common rule among public speakers.

- **Complement the stage.** Consider the stage background (especially if you will be recorded on video or photographed). If you wear a shirt that matches a backdrop, you will be hard to see. If you wear a shirt that clashes with a backdrop, you will be hard to look at.

- **Beware new fads.** Fashion trends can come as fast as they go. So don't be too trendy if you can't afford to overhaul your wardrobe often.

- **Do a last-minute check.** Before you get on stage, check yourself. Is everything zipped up, buttoned up, and in place. Are there loose hairs on your clothes? My biggest fear is preaching a sermon and realizing my zipper was down the whole time. A last-second check can stop a major embarrassment.

Fashion is always changing. So either wear classic clothes that never go out of style or update your preaching wardrobe every once in awhile.

Physical Health

We don't often think about preaching and physical fitness going together, but we need our body to preach. How we care for our body will affect our energy, confidence, and longevity in the pulpit.

As Bryan Chapell says, "You usually will preach best when well rested, physically fit, and not too recently well fed (milk products, carbonated drinks, heavy foods, and being quite full can negatively affect vocal delivery)."[78] If you have ever preached after getting no sleep, or with a bad cold you know how hard it is to preach when your body fights against you.

If we are honest, we don't talk about this very much when talking about preaching because it's taboo. A lot of preachers are not physically fit.

Most pastors are stressed, sit at their desk for long hours, eat out frequently, and don't exercise enough—including me.

My goal is not to shame anyone because they are unhealthy or overweight because I am all too familiar with the struggle myself. But we need to realize that our physical health isn't just superficial. It's a spiritual issue.

The Bible is clear that gluttony makes us lazy (Proverbs 23:20-21), and is a form of idol worship (Philippians 3:19). We should glorify God in what we eat (1 Corinthians 10:31). And our bodies belong to God, not us (1 Corinthians 6:19-20).

Paul writes, "Every athlete exercises self-control in all things. They do it to receive a perishable wreath,

---

[78]   Bryan Chapell, *Christ-Centered Preaching: Redeeming the Expository Sermon*, Kindle ed. (Grand Rapids: Baker, 2015), Location 7500.

but we an imperishable. So I do not run aimlessly; I do not box as one beating the air. But I discipline my body and keep it under control, lest after preaching to others I myself should be disqualified" (1 Corinthians 9:25-27 ESV).

Discipline in all areas—including your physical body—are required for healthy preaching. The point of being physically healthy is not just so that we would look better, although that is a nice benefit. The point of being healthy is so that we are good stewards of the body that God has given us and have the strength, energy, and longevity required to do the work God has set before us to do to the best of our abilities.

This subject can be controversial, so please know that I am not writing this in a judgmental spirit. I'm writing this more out of personal conviction.

Preaching is more than just the words we say; it's the way we live. If we want to be healthy preachers, we must be healthy spiritually, mentally, *and* physically.

Living healthier will help you be more energetic, more confident, longer living, better feeling, and yes, also better looking. There really isn't a downside to living healthier, except that it requires discipline. But discipline should be nothing new to disciples of Christ. The call of a disciple is a call for discipline in all areas of our lives.

First Impressions

Like it or not, before you ever say a word your audience will make a judgment about you based on appearance alone. Right or wrong, it's human nature.

People who have been in your church for a long time may get used to the way things are and begin to overlook appearance. But they still notice.

And first-time visitors will not miss a thing. They are analyzing everything. People will judge you on the way you dress, your age, your gender, your weight and anything else.

Most pastors think about what they communicate to the ear, but they don't always think about what they communicate to the eye. For example, people wearing glasses are often judged to be smarter, and men with bald heads are judged to be tougher. In this sense, your appearance speaks before you do.

Calvin Miller sums it up this way:

During those first critical moments when the audience to be addressed first catches sight of a speaker, the would-be listeners are making up

their minds as to whether or not they will be lis-
tening.... Each of the persons to be addressed is
sizing the preacher up with a series of questions:
Does the speaker look listenable? Is the speaker
sincere, amiable, and my kind of person? Is the
speaker dressed in a pleasing and nonostenta-
tious style? Is the speaker tattooed, dreadlocked,
gushy, friendly, aloof, etc.? First impressions
pave or bar the way to being heard.[79]

Don't allow your appearance to get in the way of your message. Although looks aren't everything, they are something you need to be aware of.

Don't obsess over your looks. Don't get caught in the snare of vanity. But be intentional about everything you communicate from the stage both to your audience's ears and their eyes.

ACTION STEP: Look At You

Look at some recent photos or videos of yourself preaching. Evaluate your appearance. Is there anything distracting or sloppy about your look? Are you

---

[79] Calvin Miller, *Preaching: The Art of Narrative Exposition* (Grand Rapids: Baker, 2006), 187.

dressed in a way that relates to the people and culture you are speaking to?

Be brutally honest. How might people judge you in a first impression based only on your appearance?

If you are fashionably challenged, like I am, get help. Find someone who knows how to dress well and ask for advice.

Identify any changes that you need to consider making.

CONCLUSION: Deliver the Gold

Listeners remember the delivery of poor speakers; they remember the content of good speakers. We communicate messages best when our delivery is transparent.... Excellent delivery disappears from the awareness of listeners. Thus, the goal of a preacher is to get out of the way of the message, to deliver the sermon so aptly that its thought alone dominates listeners' thoughts.

— Bryan Chapell[80]

---

[80] Bryan Chapell, *Christ-Centered Preaching: Redeeming the Expository Sermon*, Kindle ed. (Grand Rapids: Baker, 2015), Location 7438.

The goal of sermon delivery is to present the gospel in such a way that people only think about the message, not the messenger.

We preach the gospel—the best news ever. It's pure gold. Paul wrote, "Although I am less than the least of all the Lord's people, this grace was given me: to preach to the Gentiles the boundless riches of Christ" (Ephesians 3:8 NIV). There is no better message than the good news of Jesus Christ.

Delivering the good news in a poor way is like proposing with a diamond ring covered in mud. The value is still there, but the presentation distracts from the point. Like Paul, we ought to be grateful that God has gracefully allowed us to proclaim these riches to others.

My hope is that this book has been an encouragement to you. You can preach better sermons. You can master sermon delivery in a way that holds your audience's attention, eliminates all distraction, and leads them to them to Jesus. It takes discipline, intentionality, and practice. But don't get discouraged.

God has chosen you to be His messenger. He has given you the weighty responsibility of preaching the gospel. So give it all you've got. Don't settle for apathetic preaching. Don't be content with sloppy delivery. Don't tolerate recurring distractions that dilute a strong message.

Sermon delivery matters because we have in our possession a message of infinite worth that needs to be said, and needs to be said well.

Final Thought

There is just one overarching principle that I want to leave you with: Without God, every tip and tactic in this book is meaningless. Above all else, focus on your relationship with Him.

If God has called you to preach, He has already equipped you with everything you need. So seek Him with everything you have. Then, crack open your chest and expose your heart to your people.

Like Moses, who's face shone after spending time in the presence of God, the evidence of a strong relationship with God will be evident in you.

Charles Spurgeon urges:

We say to you, perfect yourselves in oratory, cultivate all the fields of knowledge, make your sermon mentally and rhetorically all it ought to be (you ought to do no less in such a service), but at the same time remember, "it is not by might, nor by power," that men are regenerated or sanctified, but "by my Spirit, saith the Lord.[81]

Give yourself wholly to the Lord. Speak in a way that brings glory and honor to His name. Devote yourself to delivering His message the way it deserves. Preach and deliver.

ACTION STEP: Practice How You Preach

Reading this book without practicing what you learn is like trying to learn to ride a bike by watching videos on YouTube. At some point, you can learn all the techniques and methods, but if you never get out there and fall a few times, you will never get any better.

So congratulations for finishing the book. Many people never get this far. But your journey is just getting started. Keep practicing how you preach.

If you haven't already, go to www.ProPreacher.com/Deliver to download my free sermon evaluation form. Then, pick one lesson from this book a week to

---

81   Charles H. Spurgeon, *Lectures To My Students* (Fig, 2012), 139.

focus on. Review the lesson, follow the action step, and evaluate your progress. I guarantee that the more you practice, the better you will get.

Go out there. Preach. Make mistakes. Learn from them. Preach better. Repeat.

Can You Help Me?

Hey, thanks for reading this book!

If you found it helpful, would you do me a quick favor?

Would you take a few seconds to go online to Amazon.com and leave an honest review of this book?

I personally read all the reviews. They help me know if the book is connecting with you, and how I can continue to improve.

It also helps other people discover the book and decide whether or not it's worth their time.

As an independent writer, your reviews mean the world to me.

Thanks!

- Brandon Hilgemann

Learn More

If you liked this book and would like to learn more, please visit ProPreacher.com for hundreds of free preaching articles, sermon illustrations, and more.

Also, you can always connect with me on Twitter @ProPreacher or Facebook at facebook.com/pro-preacher. Or feel free to send me an email at brandon@ProPreacher.com. I would love to hear how the tips in this book have helped you.

About the Author

Hey, I'm Brandon. Thanks for reading my book!

I'm the husband to my beautiful wife, Taryn, and father to our my two awesome kids, Ashlyn and Jaxon.

I have worked as a pastor for years in multiple churches across the country from church plants to some of the largest and fastest growing churches in the United States. And I love preaching.

For the last decade, I have been on a journey to become the best preacher I can be.

I've preached multiple sermons a week for years. I've worked in different churches absorbing everything I could. I've read every preaching book, blog post, and article I can. I've listened to thousands of sermons. And I'm still learning.

In November of 2012, I started a blog about preaching to write my thoughts from this journey and decided to name it ProPreacher.com. Then I told no one.

I was afraid what people might think. But I also wanted to see if what I wrote would even resonate with people.

I didn't want people to visit my blog because they knew me or I asked them to. I wanted people to come because the content was so compelling and helpful that they wanted to come back for more.

To my surprise, people showed up, came back, and shared it with their friends.

I'm blown away by the fact that the ideas and principles I've learned and shared on ProPreacher.com have been read by thousands of pastors around the world.

I don't pretend to be the world's foremost preaching guru. I still have a lot to learn. But my hope is that the things I've learned and continue to learn will help you as much as they have helped me.

Thanks for taking this ride with me. Keep on preaching.

– Brandon Hilgemann

Other Books by Brandon Hilgemann

Available now in physical, digital, or audio form at Amazon.com

Printed in Great Britain
by Amazon

67440869R00133